BUFFERING

ALSO BY HANNAH HART

My Drunk Kitchen:
A Guide to Eating, Drinking, and Going with Your Gut

BUFFERING

UNSHARED TALES OF A LIFE FULLY LOADED

Hannah Hart

DEY ST.

An Imprint of WILLIAM MORROW

Illustration on page 24 © Auntie M Photog

Illustration on page 73 © Cory Godbey

Jacket image on page 249 originally published in *The Charcoal Burner and Other Poems, Translated from the Chinese*, by Henry H. Hart. Copyright © 1974 University of Oklahoma Press. Reprinted with permission of the publisher. All rights reserved.

Poem on page 255, "The Uses of Sorrow," from *Thirst* by Mary Oliver, published by Beacon Press, Boston, Copyright © 2004 by Mary Oliver, used herewith by permission of the Charlotte Sheedy Literary Agency, Inc.

Watercolor images throughout the book © Art by Hannah Gelb

DEY ST.

BUFFERING: UNSHARED TALES OF A LIFE FULLY LOADED. Copyright © 2016 by Harto, Inc. All rights reserved. Printed in the United States of America. No part of this book may be used or reproduced in any manner whatsoever without written permission except in the case of brief quotations embodied in critical articles and reviews. For information, address HarperCollins Publishers, 195 Broadway, New York, NY 10007.

HarperCollins books may be purchased for educational, business, or sales promotional use. For information, please email the Special Markets Department at SPsales@harpercollins.com.

A hardcover edition of this book was published in 2016 by Dey Street Books, an imprint of William Morrow Publishers.

FIRST DEY STREET BOOKS PAPERBACK EDITION PUBLISHED 2017.

Designed by Suet Yee Chong

Library of Congress Cataloging-in-Publication Data has been applied for.

ISBN 978-0-06-245752-3

17 18 19 20 21   RS/LSC   10 9 8 7 6 5 4 3

"There are no bad guys in this story."

—MOM

CONTENTS

FOREWORD

When Hannah asked me to write the foreword to this book I was flattered and assumed she'd made a horrible mistake. Spell-check seemed equally baffled; changing "foreword" to "forward" over and over, as if even the application agreed it was an error. *Obviously she meant to ask Jennifer Lawrence*, I told myself. Or possibly J-Lo. We get each other's mail all the time. But turns out that Hannah DID mean to ask me to write her foreword and I was like "HELL YES, I WILL" because I love her. And you probably do, too, if you are reading this. Who reads the foreword? Stalkers, mostly. But that's beside the point. The point is that Hannah is amazing and also that I don't know what goes into a foreword. It sounds like a mix of "foreplay" and "words," and I think that equals "sexting," I guess? Seems a bit weird, but I am a true friend, so here goes: 8, #amIright? (8 = sideways boobies. I think? This is my first time sexting. Sorry. It's embarrassing for all of us.)

Turns out I'm not good at phone sex *or* forewords. Hang on. Let me research what a foreword is so I have a better idea of what goes here.

Okay. I'm back. According to the Internet, a foreword deals with "the purpose, limitations, and scope of the book and may include acknowledgments of indebtedness." Got it. Ignore the boobies I gave you a minute ago. I'm taking back my boobies. Let's start over.

Ahem.

When Hannah asked me to write this foreword, I said yes, but hesitantly, because I've been in a depression that's been holding on to my life for the last few months. I've started writing it several times and always erased it because my broken head hates everything about me right now. But Hannah sees past that. She sees the truth and she sees things I need to be reminded of. Like the fact that depression lies. Or that I am worthy. Or that I'll still be her friend even if I never finish writing this.

Hannah has been through some things in her life, which she talks about in this book, that could have turned her bitter, but instead they gave her a capacity for kindness and strength, and a perspective that lets me see myself and the world with new eyes. It's a gift she shares with others, and one that brings hysterical laughter or tears or both. She shares her truth with an honesty that is inspiring—one that makes me believe her when she says that it's going to get better or that laughter is just around the corner or that you aren't alone.

And I'm not. Because I have Hannah and I have her stories of pain and joy and discovery. And hope. And after you read this book, you will, too.

And that is a wonderful thing.

—Jenny Lawson

TRIGGER WARNING

Hello!

My name is Hannah Hart. Some of you may know me from my superglamorous life[1] as an Internet demigod who is so unavoidably famous and successful that it borders on the obscene. We're living in an era of such constant output via social media that all you need is a phone and a Wi-Fi connection to start creating a public persona. Got an opinion? Blog about it. Somebody said something rude? Blast 'em across all platforms. Took a cool picture of a snail? POST THAT SHIT.

Others of you may not know me at all. Maybe you've never even heard of me. But somehow you ended up holding this book. (Isn't the cover neat? What pulled you in? Was it the gold foil? As I said, SUPER-GLAMOROUS life.) And that means you are about to get to know me *really well*. Almost *too well*.

And while I am a proud social media titan operating in the age of the overshare, it's only natural that I might need some privacy too. Which is why I've never shared anything quite like this

---

1   Glamorous life = drinking Merlot and making fancy frittatas in front of a camera in my kitchen.

before. But it's not because I didn't want to. It's because I simply wasn't ready. Some things just take time to process, and one must have healthy boundaries of time and space in place in order to do so. Simply put:

BOUNDARIES + PROCESSING = BUFFERING

Buffering is that time you spend waiting for the pixels of your life to crystallize into a clearer picture; it's a time of reflection, a time of pause, a time for regaining your composure or readjusting your course. We all have a limited amount of mental and emotional bandwidth, and some of life's episodes take a long time to fully load.

You're probably wondering, "Hannah, what are these deep, dark, until now unshareable episodes you speak of?" Well, you'll have to read on to find out, but they're mostly things like:

Schizophrenia

Sexuality

Questions of faith

Questions of fame

Psychedelic visions in the desert

Self-harm

Sex

Spiders

. . . and more!

I called this introduction "Trigger Warning" because I wanted to give you guys a heads up that there won't be any other trigger warnings in this book. I did this intentionally because I don't think that there are many trigger warnings in real life. What's important is to learn how to identify what triggers you, and to set up your systems to cope after the incident has occurred. So get a cup of tea, read near a friend, or do whatever it is you do to comfort yourself should the need arise.

Now, without further ado, let's go behind the scenes (screens?) of this life that I call mine. I think I'm ready to start. And thank you for reading. Selfishly, I wanted to write this to feel less alone. Selflessly, I hope it helps you feel less alone too.

Love,

HANNAH

P.S. Follow your @harto.

The names and identifying characteristics of several individuals featured in this book have been changed to protect their privacy.

HEIRLOOM

My mom, Annette, as a young woman.

I guess we should start from the beginning.

I was born on November 2, 1986. I grew up in Burlingame, California, a city nestled into the Bay Area just south of San Francisco that smelled like roses and chocolate, divided between the affluent hills and the low-income part of town where we lived. It's called the "flat-part." Our house was by the railroad tracks and a sound wall that led to the freeway. We faced a car repair shop and could hear the almost constant noise of things being taken apart and put back together.

On Christmas Eve 1987, when I was a year old, the cops knocked on the door and took my mother, Annette, to the hospital for fourteen days because she'd had a "nervous breakdown." Some told me it was because she had called the cops saying my dad was attacking her with a knife. Others told me it was because she had attempted suicide. From that day forward the world seemed to paint my mother as an unreliable source. A liar even. Because no one could tell if what she was saying was true or not.

The truth was that she was never a liar. My mother is one of the most honest people I've ever known. My mother is so honest, in fact, that she'll tell you about the things that no one else can see or hear. She calls this her "vivid imagination," and it's what enables her to be such a talented artist. Once, as a kid, I asked her to draw me a bath. She put pen to paper, and without ever lifting the tip from the page she drew and shaded a claw-foot bathtub. I thought she was magnificent.

Between 1987 and 2003, there were fourteen incident reports filed by Child Protective Services (CPS) that led to to my younger sister and me being removed from the house.[1] In 2003, just after I turned seventeen, I was emancipated and my six-year-old half sister, Maggie, was placed into the foster system. The next year, I got into UC Berkeley, took out student loans, and was awarded some need-based scholarships so that I could attend. My life had been a case study in charity and gratitude.

However, despite all of these court cases and incidents with the authorities, nobody could tell us what was going on. Naomi and I had a theory that our mother was suffering from a disease called schizophrenia, which a quick Google search defines as "a long-term men-

---

1   Now called "Child and Family Services" to make it sound less scary.

tal disorder of a type involving a breakdown in the relation between thought, emotion, and behavior, leading to faulty perception, inappropriate actions and feelings, withdrawal from reality and personal relationships into fantasy and delusion, and a sense of mental fragmentation." Without treatment, schizophrenia spreads like a parasite through the mind devouring reality completely and leaving behind the wake of a world perforated by invisible nightmares.

But we didn't know all that yet. We just knew that Mom was "unstable" and "irrational" and just getting "weirder and weirder."

In the spring of 2007, I came home from a semester abroad in Japan to discover that my stepfather, David, had left my mother and that she was being evicted. They'd been married for eleven years. Maggie was their child, and after she'd been removed from the house four years earlier, David had tried to help Annette[2] get the medical care she needed, but she wasn't interested. She had other things on her mind. ("There is nothing wrong with me. What we should be worried about are the urban pimps that live in the phone lines!") There was nothing that David or any of us could do to get her into treatment. In the state of California it's nearly impossible to get a loved one psychiatric treatment without their consent. And since her illness separated her reality from ours, she couldn't understand what the fuss was all about.

Annette's disability meant she hadn't worked in more than ten years. David left her with enough money in savings to pay her rent for four months. I was twenty years old and working to keep myself in school. My older sister, Naomi, was twenty-four and working to live while paying off her own student loans. Neither of us could afford to keep Annette in the two-bedroom, one-bathroom house. Again, our

---

2 We call the illness "Annette" and the happy memories "Mom."

mother's concerns were elsewhere. A minor housing issue was nothing compared to disabling the transmitter that the Catholic Church had implanted in a van that parked on her street, or getting back the $1.3 trillion that the government had stolen from her, money that was her birthright as designated by her English heritage.

This meant that it was up to Naomi and me to move her out of the house. We found a residential hotel where she could stay for $640 a month. The room she had there was . . . well, it was literally a room, with a shared bathroom down the hall. It was essentially a halfway house, or rather a halfway hotel. It was decided that I would find an additional job[3] and that Naomi and I would split the rent.[4] However, you could not fit forty-eight years of memories into a single room. There was simply nowhere for everything to go. There was barely anywhere for my mom to go.

I should take a moment to tell you something: I really love my mom. When I was growing up, she was quirky and silly and fun and passionate. She loved history and mystery and art and magic and, oddly enough, miniature food-shaped erasers. Her illness has made her almost unrecognizable, but every now and then, she'll tell me that she's proud of me, and for a second I think I can see the old her behind her glassy, reddened eyes.

During her last days in that house we put everything into trash bags. Naomi and her boyfriend, Michael, pulled out photo albums and other objects that they wanted to save. My mother had a passion for rock collecting, garage sailing, archaeology, and antiquing. To her

---

3 My third. At the time I was also working at Berkeley's School of Journalism as assistant to the director of new media, and also as "maintenance manager" in the co-op where I lived, taking care of clogged sinks and toilets.

4 It was a solution that would not last long. By the time I graduated, Mom was homeless.

credit, she had accumulated some cool stuff. There was just . . . *a lot of it.*

I was twenty years old and twenty years bitter and desperate to pretend that none of that mattered to me, so I didn't save anything. Plus, I only had a single room back at school and the budding adult in me was not eager to carry around the vestiges of my childhood. My memories of cleaning out the house are a blur, and it's only now that I've begun to regret not taking anything for myself.

But I did write some things down.

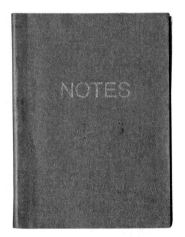

IMPORTANT THINGS

* *the green desk*

* *the rocking chair*

* *the swan box*

* *the globe*

12:38: Loses it over the dolly . . . probably my mistake.[5]

"At least I'm not a piece of human garbage!"

"Alone in this house without my children, without my husband . . ."

My fingers fall on a moldy robe, and she sees me move quickly to throw it away. I'm allergic to mold. She's not happy.

"How can you ask me to throw this away? It's good! It's clean! We have pictures of you wearing these! We were happy." She's sobbing.

"Look at this photo—Maggie is wearing the love bug robe. David is wearing his old navy medals . . . There is a lot of hope, Hannah."

It gives me no comfort to think that my irrational belief in things working out for the best in all likelihood may stem from my mother's tenuous grip on reality.

Regarding the appearance of the house alone, the level of filth, one would think that five people were living here, but the feeling of stillness, the dust, the stagnance of inactivity were inescapable markers of the truth.

I feel guilty, like I'm blowing up a museum. It's no wonder Mom can't throw any of these things away. Of course she can't. It feels like disposing of a body or packing up after a funeral. Aside from the damp breaths of mold or the soft smell of rot associated with the clothes, there are a thousand memories attached to each item: the weight and feel of Maggie as a baby, her Lion King

---

5 Annette had lost it (meaning she'd had a psychotic episode) over seeing me walk into the house with a dolly to start moving things.

---

underpants, her bonnet, her tiny socks, my tiny socks, Naomi's first job at Chickn-Chickn, can't believe Mom kept the apron, Weasley is my King T-shirt, I thought I lost this, the stains, the tears in fabric, the overuse of everything . . . overused but lasting. At a time when we had so little these clothes gave us so much. Until now. Until this moment when I throw it all into this big black bag. The reward for their tenure.

It's a silent job and there's nothing that can be said. I don't know where Naomi and Mike are. Mom's footsteps pacing/stomping above me. Her babbling is sometimes enraged, sometimes nonsensical, she's talking to no one. I picture her standing in the middle of the room, her brain reaching a wall in logic before turning around and starting to circle again.

I'm holding a black sweater with candy stuck to it. I start to pull it off to see if the candy is good to eat. I'm repulsed by my own instincts. You have other food, Hannah. Just throw the clothes in the bag.

Mom is coming downstairs as I pick up Naomi's 1920s flapper dress. This was our first store-bought Halloween costume. She looked beautiful. She fit in seamlessly at school. We were all her. We were all proud.

"Oh, leave it out so Naomi can say goodbye." She's going upstairs. I think she's talking to Naomi.

I find another garbage bag on the ground with about five items in it. She must have tried to start the process on her own and stopped. I have to stop myself from picturing her down here alone, trying to throw away her lifetime, only unable to do so. Some might say that's a good instinct. Maybe she's been saving all this stuff for so long because she was waiting for her life to start back up again. Is that hope?

Naomi and Michael are coming down to whisper.

"We got the photo albums and important books. We put them in the car. You should stop, okay? I don't even want to touch this stuff. I don't want you to touch this stuff."—Naomi

"If we're going to screw somebody, we want it to be the landlord of this house. Not your mom."—Michael [6]

"My vote is we chloroform her. Wakes up? House is empty. Bam."—Naomi is trying to make things funny.

"Hope is not a strategy, Hannah."—Michael

They are going upstairs. I hate that they aren't helping me clean. I don't know why they want to keep anything.

I find a pink princess hat. We went to Disneyland once when I was five. I got a blue princess hat. I remember breaking off the elastic because I wanted to play with it.

Mom is coming downstairs reeking of BO. She hasn't been bathing despite the shampoo and soap we brought her. She's hugging me. "You're not throwing away anything that has sentimental value, right?" She's walking away. "You know I love your stepdad."

---

6   Michael was referring to the fact that this job was simply too much for our motley crew to handle, and that we needed to focus on what was best for keeping Mom housed, rather than cleaning out her belongings.

"I know, Mom."

"Are you writing out your feelings?"

"Of course."

She's nodding. "That's what I do when I can't talk to someone I love."

She goes upstairs.

I'm stopping. I can't keep going.

Because somehow, despite everything . . . I manage to find a used condom wrapper on the ground.

Condoms make great water balloons.

I didn't grow up with a lot of toys, so as a kid I would play with anything I could get my hands on. Condoms were something I found hilarious and entertaining until the day I learned what they were really for. Then I was mildly grossed out and lost interest in them. I doubt it had anything to do with the lesbian status of my id, but who knows. Condoms weren't the only unorthodox toys Naomi and I played with as children. Since there was never adult supervision, anything we could find in the house was fair game.

One night, when I was five years old, I made a "potion" out of aspirin. I think the top of the bottle must have been broken, but when my mom told the story she always said that I could read by age five and simply read the instructions on how to open it. She believed that each of her children was a prodigy in some regard. We were all special, and brilliant. She never let us forget it. Our family was royalty, and our bloodlines could be traced back to English kings. But we also had Jewish roots. And maybe even some extraterrestrial in us, too. Did we know that we were each born lucky and each had our own superpower?

At the time it was just the three of us—my mother, Naomi, and me. She and my father had separated, and Mom was working temp jobs transcribing video recordings of newscasts. Every cent she made was put toward keeping us in this house in an increasingly expensive suburb of the Bay Area. She insisted that good schools would keep us safe. Our house was on the same block as our elementary school. As an adult I can see what incredible value this held for a single mother. Naomi and I could walk ourselves to and from school, and Mom could work whatever shift at whatever job she could find.

That night Naomi and Mom were watching TV in the living room. The show was scary, so I wandered off to find a way to entertain myself. Our house had five rooms, but we used only two and a half of them. The others were off limits. The blue bedroom had a door that was always shut. It was filled with furniture and antiques from my mother's various finds. I once broke a teacup from the blue bedroom. It was green and vaguely Irish looking. It may have been a family heirloom from my great-grandmother's[7] side. Mom was incredibly angry when she found out, apoplectic. She rarely got angry, but when she did, it was devastating. I remember running off and trying to fix the cup with Elmer's glue, crying because my fingers

---

7 My great-grandma Long was the only person who showed my mom any kindness as a kid. She died not long before this incident took place.

were sticking together but the pieces of the cup wouldn't. I felt small and useless. Mom found me and held me and wiped my tears, telling me that she was sorry, so sorry for her anger and that the cup was just a material thing. And material things didn't matter. People before objects, Hannah. Always.

Our kitchen was also in a constant state of domestic threat. I'll spare you the description. Let's just say flies and maggots and hidden rats and leave it at that.

Our dining room was where all the books and miscellaneous technology went. Keyboards without computers. Printers without paper. Piles of newspapers and magazines. The dining room was where our pets would go to defecate. There were French doors that separated it from the living room.

The second bedroom was where Naomi and I slept at night. There was a mattress on the floor and clothing, well, everywhere. As an adult who's worked with charities, I now understand why there were so many garbage bags filled with clothes around our house. And why we could never seem to find anything that fit. It's because most shelters will hand you an assorted bag of clothing vaguely marked "girls" or "boys" with an age range. It wasn't until recently that I put all of this together.

The living room was where my mother would sit up at night until she joined us in the bedroom to sleep. She would spend hours chain-smoking cigarettes and listening to Art Bell or Pastor Murray on the radio or talking on the phone to people she knew. That last sentence was a lie I told myself. The truth was that she was talking to herself.

Anyway, back to the aspirin.

I wandered down the hall toward the bathroom. One of my

favorite ways to entertain myself was to go into the bathroom and bite the lipstick out of the tube. I liked the waxy way it felt against my teeth and tongue. I spat it into the toilet and put the empty tubes under the sink. And that's where I found the aspirin. I don't know where I got the idea, probably from a medieval history show I had seen on PBS, but I decided that I was going to crush up these tiny white pills, thirty or so, and make myself a potion. They were easy to crush with the bottoms of other bottles, and if I could find a cup, I'd mix it all up with water and drink it. And that's exactly what I did.

As soon as I swallowed, I knew I'd done something wrong. It was as though a raindrop fell from the sky and through the ceiling, landing like a cold spark against the top of my head. I had just done something bad. I had done something very bad, but I didn't know what and I was starting to feel scared about it.

I calmly walked with the (now empty) aspirin bottle into the living room, where Mom and Naomi were still watching TV.

"What's this?"

My mother glanced toward me. "It's medicine. Don't eat it, it can kill you."

If before my panic had been a raindrop, I was now drenched in a thunderstorm. I don't remember what I said, but I do remember starting to wail. I was only five, but I certainly did not want to die.

My mother sprang from the couch toward me—whether she'd heard the empty bottle drop, or had simply figured things out, I'm not sure. She carried me toward the phone and called Poison Control. I remember the look on her face as she stared back at me. It sticks with you, that first memory of seeing worry—blind panic—on your parent's face. She was only a few years older than I am today, living my adultolescent[8] life and feeling so lost at times. But at least I'm not on the phone with poison control while holding my child who has just potentially killed herself.

The conversation was not going well. Mom was becoming angry with whomever was on the other end of the line. Phone calls often ended this way for her.

She told us that we had to drive to the hospital and we had to leave now. As we ran to the car Naomi threw herself down on the sidewalk out front and screamed, "Please God, don't let my sister die!" into the night. I was not thankful for her prayer in that moment. I was embarrassed.

At the hospital everything was cold and bright. Mom and the doctor were not happy to see each other. My mother had trouble getting along with a lot of adults we encountered. He was not kind, though, I could tell. I remember finding him very scary as he handed me a kidney-shaped tray and a cup full of what looked like tar. That wasn't far off; it was charcoal. He told me to drink it and I said I didn't want to. He said don't sip it, that will make it worse. Well, I wasn't going to drink it without tasting it, was I? I took a sip, and the taste made me want to cry again. Mom asked if there was an alternative to my having to drink the charcoal. He said that he could put a breathing tube through my nose and a hose down my throat to my stomach.[9] She glared at him. She hated doctors. She told me to drink it, and I did.

---

8 Adultolescent = amateur adult = the second adolescence we call "young adulthood."

9 Honestly, this guy was being such a dick. Little did he know that his statement and the image that went along with it would haunt my dreams throughout my elementary school years.

As the charcoal moved past my gag reflex and I puked everything out, my last recollection was seeing my dinner come back up and being worried that it would mean I'd have to wait until tomorrow before I ate again.

In all the years we lived as a family (a family that grew and grew and then shrank and shrank) our home was never clean. I remember reading the word "squalor" for the first time and having to look up the definition. Upon reading it my brain made a "ruh-roh" motion and pulled on my collar. Authorities came and went with threats of "clean this place up, or we'll take the children away." The cops were the enemy.

There were numerous incidents like the aspirin story during my childhood. I remember a time when I stabbed my leg with a boning knife while Naomi and I were watching a tape of *Tiny Toon Adventures*. Naomi ran to the bathroom to get a cold washcloth to press down on my leg and then had to go to a neighbor's house to call my mom at work[10] since our phone bill hadn't been paid and the phone

---

10 The rules when my mom was at work:
    1. Never call 911.
    2. Call her at work only if someone is bleeding.

had been shut off. I saw the little worms of fat splitting the skin beneath. This was my first examination of the human body. If I had to put my thoughts into words, they would be Whovian: "We are a lot bigger on the inside."

Another time, in middle school, when Maggie was still a baby, we were told that we had to clean the house or the cops would take her away. My friend Rachel's family came over to help out. I remember using a mix of bleach and ammonia to clean the bathroom with Rachel. The windows were all shut, and Rachel and I were definitely getting accidentally high. Her mom, Jane, saved us from further exposure, telling us through her laughter what idiots we were. And it was true. But we were happy idiots.

Our house was never tidy. If we're going by the standards of Child and Family Services, it was technically "uninhabitable." But it was full of happy memories and sacred objects. Even when my mother spent 2008 living out of a shopping cart, she kept the things that were most sacred to her, like Naomi's kindergarten graduation certificate with her award for "Most Improved Handwriting." My mom may not be sane, but she sure is sentimental.

I wish I hadn't been so hasty when I was twenty, shoving our memories into garbage bags in my mom's house. I regret not taking something for myself—an heirloom—whereas Naomi had the maturity and the foresight to salvage the things that were precious to her. But I suppose we can't hold on to everything. Sometimes we have to start over and make new heirlooms for our children to eventually put into their own boxes or bags as they see fit.

But from the time I was a teenager I've kept a journal. I began journaling because of my mother. Initially I thought I could make some sense of her logic by transcribing and translating her thoughts. I figured that if I didn't understand what she was saying, it was simply because I wasn't paying close enough attention. If I could crack her code and learn to speak her language, we would find a way to communicate. I spent years recording my mother's prose, word for word, and then looking for a purpose where there was none. But then eventually I found one. Because the habit of transcribing her thoughts led me to begin recording my own.

When I set out to write this book, I realized that although I didn't save anything from our old house, my heirlooms have always been with me, in the form of the memories recorded in my journals. So this chapter and those that follow, and the journals that inspired them, are my inheritance. And now I'd like to pass them down to you.

Because at the end of the day, we are all kind of one big family.

Hrm. Speaking of family, next up, my dad.

ORIGINAL KIN

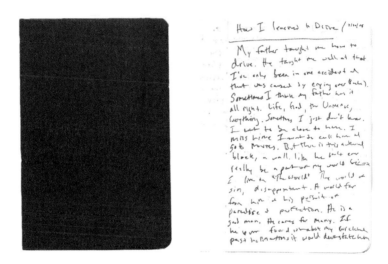

3/30/09

My father taught me how to drive. He taught me well at that.
I've only been in one accident and that was caused by crying
over Rachel. Sometimes I think my father has it all right. Life,
God, the Universe, Everything. Sometimes I just don't know. I
want to be close to him. I miss him. I want to call him and go
to movies. But there is always this awkward block, a wall. Like
he can't ever really be a part of my world because I live in "The

World." The world of sin, disappointment. A world far from him and his pursuit of perfection. He is a good man. He cares for many. If he ever found out about my wretched past inclinations it would devastate him.

I think I'm slowly becoming straight. I'm slowly leaving behind my world of women and should try harder to meet a good clean guy who is caring and sensitive and dorky. No one who smokes, no one who listens to loud music. Just someone who will love me as I try to love him. One day, maybe that can happen. Maybe when I'm more fully formed. And Dad will never have to know that I filled the car I learned to drive with women and kisses. Drove it to their homes so I could continue to explore this deviance. My dysfunction.

People have often told me that I'm "well spoken," to which I usually reply, "Why, thank you! Probably comes from my dad, Noah. He's a preacher." Then they say we must have a great relationship, and I say, "No, not really, it's actually pretty distant on account of the fact that I'm gay." Then they offer their condolences and we move along.

But this isn't a conversation, this is a book, so I'm just going to tell you the whole truth. And "The Truth" is something my dad is an expert in.

My father is a Jehovah's Witness. Witnesses refer to their religion as "The Truth" and the unfortunate realm outside of it as "The World." To me, that life seemed too isolating. And also socially irresponsible, since Witnesses don't participate in "the government of man," meaning that they don't vote. Which I think everyone should do! We owe it to our future generations to make the world better than we found it. The Witnesses were officially founded in 1931, but the religion was based on a Bible study group that started back in the 1870s. They've failed to predict the apocalypse three times (in 1914, 1925, and 1975). But hey, who's counting?[1]

My father and mother both became Witnesses in the early 1980s. They met in 1979 at age twenty-one at work. He was her supervisor, and to be honest I don't remember what the job was. But they met and quickly fell in love, marrying two years later. When I was a kid I asked my father about his first memory of meeting my mother. I was hoping to hear something about her interests or hobbies, something I could attach a sense of lineage to. His reply was, "When I went to pick her up for our first date, she made me wait outside for a long time. Then when I walked in, there were towels everywhere covering up stacks of dirty dishes. Very strange. There was a lot of tin hat stuff happening back then, too."

By "tin hat stuff" he was referring to "the wearing of a tin hat to keep alien radio waves out of your head," a phrase sometimes used to describe the behavior of people with paranoia. I think. Schizophrenia first manifests in the early twenties. So my mother was probably starting to hear voices for the first time when she and my father met. Due to the stigma surrounding schizophrenia and a general lack of awareness back then, there was no way that my father could have known that. And also no way he could have known that someone with borderline psychosis needed to stay as far away from psychedelic drugs as possible.

Too bad that's exactly what he was into at the time.

It's hard for me to imagine what my dad must have been like before he joined the Witnesses. But here are some of the things I do

---

1 I am.

know: he went to a special school for gifted kids, graduated from high school at the age of sixteen, and was accepted into the budding Computer Science program at UC Santa Cruz. This was in the 1970s, before most people realized how important computers would become. He was asked to join MENSA, and because of his early work on computer programming, he was at the forefront of all the technology we build our lives on today.

Other things I know: his father was an alcoholic, and my dad was the second in a line of five siblings. He studied tai kwon do and was "the fun brother" who smoked a lot of weed and did harder drugs. He also briefly dabbled in Buddhism. With black-brown hair, blue eyes, a big smile, and a broad build, he was always well liked by those around him. A charming, intelligent, funny Jewish boy—until he was no longer Jewish. He said a rabbi once told him, "You don't need to believe in God to be Jewish," and that was the end of it for him. Incredibly ironic, considering the many contradictions of his chosen faith. But hey. To each their own.

When he met my mom he was still in his "Let's do drugs and try to contact spirits" phase. She pulled him out of that and into another form of mind control. She had recently met a Jehovah's Witness, who invited them to join a Bible study group to lead them away from the confusing world and toward the blissful opportunity of eternal life on a paradise earth. That sounded pretty good to both of them.

In 1983 they had Naomi, and in 1986 they had me. After I was born, Annette started to pull away from the religion and had relations with another man. Noah did the same (with a woman). They eventually divorced, were "disfellowshipped"[2] by the Witnesses, and

---

2 Meaning they were cast out from The Truth as unrepentant wrongdoers. You can be disfellowshipped for any act that goes against Watchtower doc-

later they reconciled. Noah insisted that they try to be "reinstated" in the Truth, but Annette didn't want to be. Noah was eventually reinstated, but Annette never was. However, they got very close to being remarried; in fact, they tried to get remarried twice, but Annette was against the religion and constantly flip-flopping about their marriage. The last time they tried, they drove to Nevada in the night (with my sister and me in the backseat) and made it all the way to the judge's chambers with marriage license in hand before Annette suddenly said she needed a cup of coffee and never came back. The judge laughed at my dad and said he wasn't going to be marrying them any time soon.

So that's enough background on Noah the person; let's move on to talking about Dad.

Growing up, Naomi and I would spend four days a month with our father at his home across the bay in Fremont. "Dad Weekends" could be nice, but if our visit fell on a holiday, we were screwed. Jehovah's Witnesses don't believe in celebrating holidays of any kind, including birthdays, because they are pagan. They explain this by reciting a parable about John the Baptist, who was killed as a birthday present to King Herod. Thus, all holidays are evil and sinful and pagan. Duh. The end.

If a "Dad Weekend" fell on something big, like one of our birthdays or Christmas, my mother would do everything in her power to get him to switch. But honestly, I think that my dad still resented my mother for breaking his heart and dragging him through her "nervous breakdowns" and "emotional roller coasters." Let's all take a moment to have compassion for my father as a young man. He

---

trine as dictated by the governing body. Including things like getting a divorce from an abusive partner, being gay, and so on.

really couldn't handle how unstable my mother was. I'm sure it was traumatizing for him. He once told me about seeing her on the bathroom floor stroking razor blades along her skin. How could a man in his twenties be expected to deal with that? He simply couldn't.

But his two daughters? Sure, they could handle it. After all, he was paying her child support.

Dad had remarried, and his new wife, Jenny, who was eleven years younger than him, was also a Witness. They didn't want to have any children together. Jenny was the antithesis of Annette: no interest in anything outside of the known universe, impeccable cleaning habits, and *very* practical about money. Jenny loved thrift stores and was just a very frugal person in general. She really could make the most of a dollar, and their home looked like a page from a Pottery Barn catalogue. Saving up for vacations was also something Jenny was always good at. Meanwhile, my mom liked to come home with a $50 rock she'd found at a garage sale, but she would point out that it *could* have potentially been a Native American artifact.[3]

I don't want to spend this whole chapter unloading about my father, really. So I'm just going to share this list of things I remember about Dad Weekends, so we can get through the bad and move on to the good:

* Arriving at his house and being told that we needed to bathe.

---

3   We used to have two obsidian arrowheads my mom had found when she was a child. Those are gone now, lost in the fire of her illness and homelessness, but I think about them a lot.

* Being told not to steal the hairbrushes.

* Being told not to take the clothing in the drawers.

* Being told not to take our toothbrushes with us.

* Being told we used too much toilet paper.

* Overhearing Jenny question my intelligence because I hadn't known what a navel orange was. (In my defense, I'd had little exposure to fresh fruit.)

* Hearing Naomi called "a liar" and "hysterical like your mother" every time she "acted out," which was really just her feeling things.

* Dad locking Naomi out of the house when she refused to attend an all-day Witness Convention. Naomi sat outside for hours before she eventually called Mom from a pay phone and David (our stepdad) went to pick her up.

* Being told I was the good one.

In truth, I wasn't being good out of love or respect for their parenting. I was being good because I was kind of scared of them. Scared and ashamed for being dirty and dumb. My dad referred to me as "quiet" for most of my elementary years. I was always trying to hide to see if anyone would notice I was gone.

Naomi, on the other hand, really wanted our father's love. She adored him. I mean, look at this photo!

If that's not a photo of a child who loves her daddy, I don't know what is. Meanwhile, I'm the one on the left. I was not a smiley kid. I'm a much happier adult.

Anyway, Naomi wanted Dad to understand her. To know her. To choose her over his religion. So she fought *with* him to fight *for* him. Which led to a lot of conversations in which Naomi would cry tears of frustration as she tried to explain the logical loopholes of the religion that could maybe, one day, lead to Dad leaving The Truth and loving her again. They would debate until Jenny came and told them to stop. Then Jenny would take Dad into the bedroom to talk with the door shut and the radio on so we couldn't eavesdrop. Not that we ever even tried to, frankly.

Because of that, I knew they couldn't deal with both of us being upset, so I played along, bit the insides of my cheeks until they bled, and gnawed on the sleeves of my clothing until I was told to stop. I was the good one.

At night we would listen to "drama tapes" which were audio recordings of Bible stories, complete with divine justice and people's cries for salvation. As a child who already had night terrors, the drama tapes probably made things worse. But boy could I recite tales from the Bible and the morals that went with them! At night when I'd hear crickets outside it reminded me of the Ten Plagues.[4] What if the wrath of Jehovah was about to come down and consume us all? Shouldn't we at least tell Mom that this was coming?

I still have trouble sleeping today, but I don't think about the apocalypse anymore.

Most of the time.

Anyway, weekends with Dad were confusing. On the scale of good and evil, Jenny and Dad were the good guys, right? I mean, the power in their house never went off, their home was always kept pristine (like, don't put your cup down because it will immediately be whisked away into the dishwasher level of clean), and there was always food in the fridge that we could ask for permission to eat.

Meanwhile, despite the squalor and the chaos, I felt more comfortable at home with Mom than I ever did at my Dad's. Sure, we didn't have much, but what we did have was shared. Resources were never just for one.

Let me lighten things up a bit by telling you the things I'm grateful for:

He gave us quarters for good grades, which turned into bills as we got older. He started my first bank account for me and taught me how to build savings (something that would be invaluable in my years to come). He taught me about credit. He encouraged me to take out loans so I could go to college. He played chess with me. He played

---

4   Moses, Pharaoh, Egypt, Deliver Us, etc.

cards with me. He gave me sips of his Scotch. He took us camping with his sisters. He taught me how to pitch a tent and build a fire.

And he taught me how to drive.

Torrential.

There was no other way to describe the weather.

We were in a heavy downpour surrounded by semitrucks, and sweet Jesus, we were screwed. We were torrentially screwed.

That was my train of thought as I drove along the two-lane highway in the Sierra Nevadas. The rain poured down in thick sheets that looked like fog. I drove on the side that hugged the mountain itself, while the other lane, the "fast lane," ran the edge of the cliff above steep rocky hills.

Dad, Jenny, and I were on our way to Yellowstone National Park for what was to be my high school graduation present from my father. Naomi hadn't been allowed to come on this trip because my father had made it explicitly clear that this trip was "just for Hannah." All very lovely except for the fact that I—Hannah—wanted Naomi there.

"No, you don't. You're just so easily influenced by your sister," Jenny had said when I protested the arrangement.

"Yeah, but I—"

"Look," my father began, in a tone that indicated the conversation was ending, "Naomi had her trip to Lassen, and this drive to Yellowstone is just for you. Plus, we will get your learner's permit hours checked off so that you can have your driver's license before you go to Berkeley in the fall."

"Okay, but I didn't go on the Lassen trip because I didn't *want* to go."

"Right, and didn't you always regret it?"

"Kind of . . ."

The trip in question was part of the annual court-ordered two weeks we spent with our dad each summer. One year, when I'd still been in middle school, the plan was to go on a trip to Lassen, but I'd refused to go when I was told we'd have to attend meetings[5] while we were on the trip. It was the only bout of stubbornness I'd ever shown. Meetings were absolutely mind-numbing torture for me at that age, especially after Jenny had decided that I could no longer sleep or doodle during the talks and I had to sit still and "just pay attention." So the three of them had taken the Lassen trip without me. That's why Naomi was not allowed to come on my Yellowstone graduation trip, even though we both begged for her to go. Makes sense, right? See how that's fair? Nope? Good.

And now I, a student driver with only a learner's permit, was driving through flooded roads alongside a cliff with two semis swaying ominously before us. My freeway driving was the most limited. This was going to be the time I would learn, and I had to learn fast.

"Noah, I really don't think Hannah should be driving. Can you please take over?" Jenny once again asked in a shaky voice from the backseat, her faith in my driving as tenuous as my own.

"Jennifer, there is no safe way for us to pull off. We have to get through this pass. End of subject," my father replied without emotion. She was not to bring it up again. "Hannah, you're doing fine."

"Okay." I was quiet. At least my focus was at its best in these

---

5 "Meetings" are what Witnesses call their religious services.

types of situations. With adrenaline coursing through my body, it was easy for me to pay total attention to the task at hand.

"There are fifteen miles left of curves, and then it will straighten out."

"Okay."

"But you need to pass this truck ahead of you, understand? You're in the blind spot of that truck in the left lane, and if they move over to the slow lane they will not see us. This lane is no longer safe."

Fuck fuck fuck fuck. I had to make a left-hand pass around the tilting truck in front of me. With my windshield wipers operating at maximum speed, the spray from the tires of the truck were making it even harder for me to see.

"Are you sure? I mean, is it better for me—"

"You need to pass the truck. An opening is coming up. Check your mirrors, and when I say go, make your move."

"Okay." If I could have felt my hands, I'm sure they would have been cold and sweaty. But I couldn't feel them; all I could feel was the urgent need to get this right.

"You cannot pass on a curve. The road will straighten briefly before the next curve starts." His voice was calm and soothing and firm. It was gentle but left no room for argument or interpretation. This was the way our father instructed us when there wasn't a discussion to be had. I remember once, when I was very small, looking at the moon as we drove across the Bay Bridge to his house for the weekend. I had just started learning about space and was old enough to slightly grok the gravity of, well, gravity. I remember staring at the Moon thinking about how it orbited the Earth from such a distance in the sky when suddenly I felt like my linear brain had reached a point of non-comprehension. The distance between the Moon and the Earth was incredible and yet here I could see it outside the window of this car, reflecting against the surface of the water. I felt like the Universe was trying to squeeze inside my mind and wouldn't fit. The light reflecting off the Moon that was traveling through time at a speed I couldn't understand. It made me feel scared, itchy, and panicked. Suddenly I thought about death. I asked my father "Hey Dad, if there is no Jehovah, what happens to us when we die?" and he replied by asking "Remember what it was like before you were born?" to which I said "No," and he said "Exactly. Without faith in Jehovah death is just like that. Less than nothing."

I was quiet for the rest of the drive across the bridge. His answer had scared me more than my question.

On this drive along the mountain though, I could tell he was scared too, by the way he was sitting. Completely still and at full attention. He was in vigilance mode, trying to instruct me while also keeping an eye out for hazards. Maybe he was scared of dying, too.

But despite the danger of the conditions around us, I felt safe. It was nice. Nice to share the same feeling for a moment, even if the feeling was terror. I felt as though we were bonding. It was a glimpse of the way things might have been if our lives had been different and—

"Go."

"What?"

"Hannah. GO."

When I glanced in my mirrors, I saw that Jenny was praying. Operating on pure muscle memory, I changed lanes. Signal was on, check the mirrors, check the blind spot, and go.

The spray from the two trucks before us made the windshield opaque. We'd hit a patch of road covered in fog, we were surrounded in a cloud of white, and for a moment things seemed almost serene. Time felt still. Peaceful.

When the fog cleared, the truck in front of me—as my father had predicted—opted to change lanes into the spot I had previously occupied. It was a good thing we moved when we did.

When my dad saw this, he shouted an enthusiastic "Yes!" and clapped his hands together, laughing. "Well done."

I smiled, but I still had twelve miles of curvy road ahead of me before I could really celebrate. Still, with that maneuver under my belt I felt more confident about simply staying in my lane and inside the lines.

"Remember, never adjust your angle when taking a curve. When they design roads, they don't adjust the angle of the curve midturn, so you shouldn't, either. Brake going into it, gas coming out."

"Um, duh," I joked, feeling it was okay to resume light conversation.

I could tell he was smiling from the way his voice sounded. And then he said the words every child wants to hear.

"You're doing a good job, honey. I'm proud of you."

This is my favorite photo from that trip. It reminds me of the man who taught me to navigate the road no matter the storm. Unfortunately, he was also the man who sent me out into the proverbial storm while he looked the other way. There were one too many trials by fire and far too much accountability placed on my shoulders and my sister's when we were young. Still, we grew up to be women who were strong and confident with a deep sense of worth and self-respect.

Which is probably why we don't talk to him very often.

But this photo reminds me of happy times with my father. It reminds me of my father the teacher, my father the leader, my father the man who told me "good job." I choose to remember these moments and focus on what was given instead of what wasn't. Gratitude.

Unfortunately, despite all the ways I've accepted the person he is, his religion prevents him from accepting the person that I am. You know—a gay person. Like his father before him.

The last time I saw him was at my cousin's wedding. One of his sisters asked me why I don't talk to him and I brushed it off telling the smaller truths: that it's hard to be close to someone who thinks your love is perversion, hard to be close to a father who will never attend your wedding or call your children his grandchildren. And then I say that while he's not proud to be the father of a gay person, I do know he takes pride in my success. He's proud of the things I've accomplished, the choices I've made for my professional life, the path I've decided to pursue.

In honor of that, let's fast-forward and talk about the roads that got me to where I am today.

A different sort of highway.

The Internet superhighway. 😎 ✌️

MY DRUNK KITCHEN

N ow that you know a bit about where I come from, let's talk about where I am today! I am living the millennial dream, a demigod of digital influence, wildly self-indulgent, rich beyond all imagination, bathing in pools of gold and resting my head against pillows of money, an indomitable force who laughs in the face of traditional media, holding rank as General in the battle of dawning digital era!!!!

In other words, I'm a YouTuber.

The life of a YouTuber[1] is hard to describe because there are so many different types of YouTubers. Sure, there are similarities among us, but our styles of content are all different. There are some of us who vlog and others who simply want to teach you "50 ways

---

1   I actually prefer the term "content creator," because at this point in my career there are all kinds of different content that I create. But at the beginning, yes, I was exclusively a YouTuber.

to tie a knot." (It's fascinating how many knots there are. Please go to YouTube and search for knot tying immediately.)

It's my belief that people "who do YouTube" do it for the ability to *share*. They love sharing their knowledge, their opinions, their expertise, their experience. The format can be anything from comedy to consumer review to the casual observance of someone's daily life. This is because YouTube itself is a tool, not a type.

Now, maybe you're thinking that anyone who can make a career out of this kind of obsessive sharing must be a complete narcissist. I think this perception has something to do with the types of videos that do well online. Before we go further, here's a brief tutorial:

TAG: When a content creator makes a video in response to being "tagged" and then "tags" others to do so in turn. Example: the TMI tag: a video in which you answer twenty-five questions about yourself, ending with a list of people you are tagging whom you would also like to answer the same questions. Tag. They're it. Get it?

CHALLENGE: This type of video involves a game that you play by yourself or with a friend. The most popular challenge to date is the "Cinnamon Challenge," in which the creator attempts to eat a tablespoon of cinnamon on camera. This seems terrifying to me, and I will never do it. I did, however, really enjoy the Whisper Challenge, which involves wearing headphones and trying to read someone's lips—with hilarious results.

Person A (whispering): He was wearing a top hat.

Person B (shouting over headphones): YOU WANT TO MEET TOM PETTY!?

HAUL: I think of "haul" videos as the CNET of YouTube. In a haul, a person purchases a bunch of goods or products that they have been wanting to try. They then open and try each product, giving the viewer their immediate review. (Example: This lipstick says "smudge-proof." Let's test that. Oh, look, it works! Or not.)

VLOG: Vlogging is kind of like self-produced reality TV. A vlog can be a video about a specific topic, but lately it more commonly refers to someone video logging random events from their day. This is very popular but a little too voyeuristic for my tastes. But then I don't like to watch reality TV shows with people yelling at each other about their life choices. That's just my preference.

HOW-TO: This one is self-explanatory: people show you how to do things.[2]

LET'S PLAY: Pretty exclusive to gaming, these are videos where you watch people play video games and listen to their commentary. It's a lot like watching sports on TV, for hard-core gamers.

SCRIPTED/SKETCH: Very popular in the comedy vertical. Basically, the creator writes and films a sketch and then posts it online. There are even some popular scripted series based on literature, like *The Lizzie Bennet Diaries*, which did so well that it won an Emmy.

RANT: Somebody looks into a camera and talks about the

---

2 So many kinds of knots!! I'm telling you! It's amazing!

things that bother him or her. I think. Wait, is a rant a Wog? I don't know. Let's move on.

Now you know a little more about YouTubers.[3] Are we all work-addicted egomaniacs? I guess that's a matter of opinion. Is this career of constant output healthy or sustainable? Who knows. All I know is that this is the best job I've ever had. And I've had some pretty shitty jobs. Literally! Let's take a peek at this excerpt . . . from my journal during my years in college as maintenance manager of Hoyt Hall.

11/19/08
AN ENTRY REGARDING A SUPREMELY CLOGGED TOILET

Lately, I've lost my desire to deal with shit. I mean that quite literally. No part of me wants to fix this mess. Instead, I've chosen to let it fester and build bacteria. Why? Part of it is most assuredly laziness. The other part is a fear—no, fear is too strong—a lack of desire to deal with the festering pile. I don't want to look at it head on, I don't want it to see me. I don't want to try, and I don't want to fail at it. I don't want to touch the filthy tools used for encounters with home waste. I just want to keep the door shut and pretend it isn't there. Assure those who encounter it that I have a planned course of action in mind—simply so that they will leave me alone and I can ignore the problem too. The longer I wait the worse it will

---

3   If you still want more, I strongly recommend an *incredibly* popular and thought-provoking series called *My Drunk Kitchen*. Watch now at YouTube .com/Harto! Like and subscribe!

get. Maybe the toilet will forget the feeling of clean running water. Maybe it will figure that something pure used to exist inside and it wasn't always brimming with dung. I'm not helping the process any. The toilet used to have a clean and efficient system for renewing itself. I've taken that away. The only way to give it back is to sift through the sewage and let it sing.

Yikes.

I've included this little ditty from a dirtier time to show you that I wasn't always living the dream. Most jobs I've had in my life have not been glamorous, and I took them because they paid the bills.

(I'd also like to point out that most of my motivation for work was using guilt as a whip to drive me forward. It was the only way I knew how to discipline myself. In this journal entry I'm literally telling myself that I'm *hurting a toilet* by not cleaning it. Christ, baby Hannah. Give your baby brain a break!)

My Drunk Kitchen was different, of course. It was not a show born out of obligation or even ambition.

It began as a show about friendship.

I dunno, dude. I just . . . I just wish I could get it together, ya know?"

My friend Hannah Gelb was sniffling from the other side of the country, her tears pixelated by the quality of the web camera on my laptop. Although by March 2011 a crying Hannah Gelb was a familiar sight, it was always a painful one for me to see.

Hannah and I first met while studying abroad in Japan. The program we had both been accepted into was a partnership between the UCs (University of California) and Tsuru Bunkadaigaku (a small liberal arts college in a town nestled in the foothills of Mount Fuji). Hannah was from UC Santa Cruz, which is kind of the younger and equally hippy-dippy sibling of UC Berkeley, where I went.

Jewish and naturally neurotic, Hannah has the voice of a Disney character and a Muppet combined, which is appropriate since she sort of embodies the joyous optimism of a Disney tale paired with the soulful quality of Jim Henson's creatures. We were a perfect pair of misfits joined at the hip during our time in a foreign land.

While in Japan, my friendship with Hannah was crucial to my survival. I was in the throes of my first heartbreak and subsequent depression. I was unable to eat or motivate myself, but the friendship I formed with Hannah helped me dig myself out of that dark spiral. It wasn't her words of wisdom or spiritual guidance . . . it was our laughter that healed me. Since then, no matter how dark the days, Hannah Gelb never fails to make me laugh.

After college Hannah, her boyfriend Alex and I all headed for San Francisco and decided to be roommates in an apartment we found on the outskirts of Noe Valley. We lived together for almost a year before I announced that I had to get out of San Francisco and move to New York.[4] Hannah was happy for me but also mournful because she had counted on me for her daily pick-me-ups as she battled her (not yet diagnosed) chronic depression. There had been many tearful conversations at our kitchen table in San Francisco. So many, in fact, that it became a running joke. I'd walk into the kitchen and see her sitting staring out the window with a pile of used tissues in front of her. I'd usually say something like "Before we dive into the meaninglessness of life, do you know if we have any milk left?"

Hannah would laugh her big, joyous laugh before replying with something like "I dunno, dude, I think I used it all up on my morning cup of sorrow."

"Did you say 'morning' like daytime or 'mourning' like sad time?"

"Both."

"Perfect."

I worried a great deal about my sweet friend when I left for New York. I imagined a parallel universe where I'd stayed by Hannah's side, as her crutch, helping her to avoid emotional pitfalls wherever they appeared. But I decided that positive self-action was important, so I went. I missed her badly, but I never regretted it.

One day, a few months after I'd moved, I was down in DC cat sitting for Naomi while she and her husband attended a wedding. Naomi and her husband lived in a basement apartment with no windows and an odd dampness to it, with a fat cat named Mochi who would sit and stare at you for hours, assessing your character flaws and quietly judging you. At least that's what it seemed like to me.

---

4   More on what spurred this decision in the chapter "Fear and Ecstasy."

That night, Hannah and I were video chatting to test out the new laptop that Naomi had just gotten for me as an "I love you, please let me get you something you need"–type present. Naomi was always catching me neglecting myself, and carrying around my old, broken twenty-pound Toshiba laptop was something she'd considered neglectful. So what if it shut off randomly and had no battery life? It still turned on-ish sometimes!

"Everything just seems really hopeless. Like, am I ever going to get a real job? I work part-time, dude. At a coffee shop. Is this going to be my life forever?" Hannah sniffled.

"There's no such thing as forever, man! It's just right now. And right now you work at a coffee shop and you're learning how to be an awesome barista. We love coffee shops! That's cool!" I said.

"I don't feel cool."

"Dude. You *are* cool."

"No. You're cool. You're like the coolest. I mean, you moved to NEW YORK."

"Yeah, it is pretty cool." I liked to be jokingly smug because it made Hannah laugh. "But I also had to get surgery because I had a cyst. A cyst on my butt, Hannah! My butt!"

"That cyst was so lucky to be on your butt! I wish I was that cyst!"

"Oh, my god, then we'd really be soul-cyst-ahs!" Hannah and I were both laughing now. That was what we did. We just laughed our way through the tears. Cry. Laugh. Cry. Repeat.

Hannah was wiping tears from her eyes. "I really do miss you, man. I miss laughing like this. I miss just, like, normal stuff. Daily stuff. Ugh. I just wish you were here in my kitchen with me! Just, like, getting drunk and cooking and talking about life."

"I'm a terrible cook."

"Yeah, but you give great advice!"

"Maybe, but that's got nothing to do with cooking. Remember when I grew the Genmai Monster[5] in Japan and Erin had to wear a hazmat suit to clean it out of my rice cooker??"

"YES!!! And she drew that comic about it!!! Hahaha! That was amazing!!" Hannah paused in the middle of her laughter and was suddenly pensive.

"I was just thinking . . ." Hannah began, ". . . why did she do that for you? Did she lose a bet?"

"Huh. You know, I don't remember . . ."

The conversation was winding down and I could sense Hannah's mood starting to shift. That's the thing about joy and sorrow: they are opposite sides of the same coin. One as powerful a feeling as the other, but until Hannah found a space between them she'd be flipping back and forth. Not wanting her to become sad again, I tried to think of something I could do that would cheer her up and get her through the night. "Hey, dude, maybe you're onto something . . ."

"What do you mean?"

"Maybe I should make you a cooking show! I can just record it on this thing and cut it together and then send it to you!"

"HAHAHA! That would be AMAZING." Hannah was excited. I was excited, too. "Do you know how to do stuff like that?"

"No, but I'm sure I can figure it out. This laptop that Naomi just got for me is amazing. It's got a movie editor and music editor and all sorts of things. I can't believe computers come with this stuff!"

---

5 When I was living in Japan, I had a bad habit of making brown rice (*genmai*) and then forgetting about it—for like a month.

"You're rich!"

"SO rich."

That was a joke because at the time we were both totally broke. Although I'm tempted to point out that I was broke because I'd just spent my savings on moving to New York. I was typically obsessive about saving money. While in Japan I kept a detailed tally of all my spending because I wanted to have enough left when I got home to try to buy a used car.

Whereas my dear, sweet Gelb . . . literally spent all of her money on ice cream.

"I'm serious, man. I'm gonna do it!" I was excited.

"Really?"

"Yeah, dude, really! But you have to promise to start using your Twitter!" A year previously I had convinced Hannah to join the up-and-coming social site called Twitter. I'd joined it in 2008 and thought that if I made a funny enough account some website like McSweeney's might hire me to write for them. It was my big dream.

"I'm stoked. I'm gonna go and film it right now, before I change my mind. Wait. Lemme make sure Naomi has some wine in the apartment . . . Okay, solid, she does."

"Awesome. That's the best part."

I was confused. "What's the best part?"

"The best part of staying at your sister's place! The wine is always free," Hannah joked.

I laughed and said, "I'm using that in the video."

And I did.

The next morning Hannah sent me an e-mail:

Date: May 16, 2011
Hannah Gelb
to Hannah Hart

I think I have to realize that being 27 and not having done my thing yet is not the catastrophe it seems to be.

Let me know if you want to talk more about grad school or anything :D

DUDE, I went to the library today and looked at pictures of Morocco. it's BEAUTIFUL!!!!

Love, Gelb

Date: May 16, 2011
Hannah Hart
to Hannah Gelb

online?? i have something to show youuuu!

I had filmed the video as soon as we'd ended our video chat, and I'd edited and uploaded it the morning after (*My Drunk Kitchen*—still available to watch now on youtube.com/harto!). My motivation was simply my desire to see Hannah smile. And smile she did. She smiled so much that she shared it with all of her friends to make them smile. And then those friends shared it with all of their friends to make *them* smile. And so on and so forth. A mere forty-eight hours later, I was a viral sensation.

I'm going to skip the details of what happened after that, because at this point the whole "viral video turned YouTube star thing" is old news. But in a nutshell:

* I made some more videos.

* Those videos also went viral.

* I thought, "This could get me one step closer to my dream of becoming a writer!"

* I slept on couches to cut expenses and sold merch[6] until I had built a tiny online empire.

Making *My Drunk Kitchen* for Hannah Gelb felt amazing. When I'm creatively stuck or filled with doubt about what content I should create, or bothered by the views on videos being low, I like to take a step back and remember why this all happened in the first place: to give a friend a break from the worries of the world.

I may not have always wanted to be famous, but I have always wanted to brighten someone's day. To brighten their view of the world.

And for all of us, I think, that's the view that matters most.

---

6 Big secret: Ads on YouTube rarely pay the bills, but selling T-shirts and wristbands and coffee mugs sure does. To everyone who bought something from me in 2011–2012: THANK YOU—YOU ARE DIRECTLY RESPONSIBLE FOR WHERE I AM TODAY. THANK YOU. BLESS YOU.

HELLO, HARTO?

2011 was an amazing year. It was the year that *My Drunk Kitchen* was born, and it was the year I discovered that I had the chance to earn a living by making people feel good and laugh. My goal had always been to make enough money to support my family, and who makes more money than people in the entertainment industry! If I could figure out how to swing this into a larger career in *that* space, well, that could really be something.

But in 2011, it was anyone's guess. There were some things that people knew were effective for building a YouTube following (calls to action like asking people to subscribe, and so on), and in building relationships with other creators and researching other channels, I started to piece together a system. These days there are actual "playbooks" and "best practices" available for every form of social media, but back then there wasn't anything like that. It was all uncharted territory, which was my favorite kind.

Growing up, I was always bored in math class because finding the answers involved using equations that everybody knew. Math, it seemed, was less about problem solving and more about applying existing systems. Snooze fest. I wanted to do something different. The early years of my career were less about being an "entertainer" and more about being an "entrepreneur."

And what's more enticing than doing something that's never been done? What could be better for a naïve and ambitious heart at twenty-four?

I was determined to swing this burgeoning YouTube thing into a career. And it seemed as if that was a real possibility. *My Drunk Kitchen* was getting more and more popular, and the channel was growing into other shows as well. With interest building, I thought that there was sure to be big money in this new form of entertainment. And any amount was going to be more than what I was making as a part-time/night-working proofreader.

So 2011 was an awesome, exciting year. It felt like possibility was a light shining through me in radiant and varying color.

2012, however, was all shades of gray.

Because in February 2012, I moved to Los Angeles.

I left my couch-surfing life in New York behind and found a shared room in Silver Lake. I started to take meetings with agents who introduced me to production companies and studios in a series of meetings called "generals."[1] I was excited to figure out what Entertainment!Hannah looked like.

---

1 A "general" is a sit-down meeting with a producer or another form of creative exec that basically feels like going on a blind date over coffee during the day. It can be a pleasant enough way to spend an hour, but unless there's a spark and the timing is right, there's not much incentive to meet again. Then, if you ever see that person walking down the street, you both smile and try to remember where you met.

This is how those meetings would generally go. The first sentence out of the mouth of every executive or representative I met with was: "Picture this . . . what if . . . *My Drunk Kitchen* . . . WAS A TV SHOW?!?!?!?!?!!"

When I asked how they thought *My Drunk Kitchen* would look as a TV show, they'd immediately start morphing the format: "Well, you couldn't actually drink. And you'd probably need to make the food look at least edible. And maybe you could interview celebrities! Don't you want to meet celebrities?"

First of all, I was not a professional chef. Nor was I a polished host. Nor did I know if "hosting" was something I was able to do. What would be my stance? What would be my voice? What if I sucked? I had no training and no experience. I was nervous to try.

Second, and maybe it's because I grew up with limited access to pop culture, but the "opportunity to meet celebrities" had never enticed me personally. Except for meeting Patrick Stewart or Beyoncé or Oprah. Still hoping to make that happen.

When I told them I wasn't interested in a TV show, the response was "Are you sure? You know what, how about you just sell us the rights to *My Drunk Kitchen* and someone else can star in it? You might even get a couple thousand dollars for it!"

"No thank you," I'd say, "but I do think it would make a fun parody cookbook."

Blank stares. "Right. A book. That's a thing. Listen, I'm gonna level with you. People only have good ideas *once*. You should probably capitalize on this right now. If you don't, well, be prepared to have missed a massive opportunity."

So traditional media was telling me to sell the idea and move on, and the advice I was getting on the digital side usually went something like this:

"I love *Drunk in the Kitchen*! A drunk channel! A channel about being a drunk! That's hilarious."

To which I'd reply: "Actually, the channel is called Harto, which is my nickname. But I want it to stand for something more. And, yes, the most popular show on the channel is called *My Drunk Kitchen* but I don't want to get stuck drinking for th—"

"*My Drunk Kitchen*! Even better. And you can turn that into *My Drunk Gaming* or *My Drunk Skateboard* or *My Drunk . . . Drunk*! Just getting drunk is superfunny. Let's make sure all those channels are available first. Also, we should turn on copyright infringement settings to make sure no one is stealing your idea and making their own version."

"Actually, I don't wanna do that. I like it when people are inspired by my work to make their own videos. It's just an idea. People can do what they want with it."[2]

Then I'd offer up ideas I had that nobody seemed to be interested in or knew what to do with: like a concept for a superhero series[3] my friend Hannibal and I wanted to make, the dream of selling a book, a project involving music, and so on. But everything I suggested was either "not new enough" or "too new" to be a surefire win.

Then the meeting would end, and I'd take my overstuffed backpack (I still hadn't broken my New York City habit of traveling with everything I could possibly need at any possible moment) and either wait for the bus or drive my friend Erica's car back to where I

---

2 I've always been a big believer in sharing ideas. The magic is not in the "what" of the idea, it's in the "how." Because honestly, no one can steal your ability to come up with new thoughts.

3 A couple years later I sold that idea to Nerdist, which sold it to Legendary Entertainment, and we turned it into a modern reboot of Sid and Marty Krofft's *Electra Woman and Dyna Girl*! It was great. Kicked-butt to make it. I mean, who doesn't wanna be a superhero?

was staying, depending on the day. Entertainment!Hannah wasn't glamorous, really. Except for the fancy lunches. People seemed very interested in meeting me over meals, and that really rocked.

But above all else what really got me down about LA was the city's lack of walkability. That had a real effect on my mental health. I missed walking around the city observing lives outside my own. Long story short, I missed New York.

APRIL/MAY 2012

I will have a deeper and personal relationship with my life. I will not have a casual fling with my life. I need to work for a purpose greater than myself. I will find peace in that. I want to contribute to the world around me. Casual debauchery is not fulfilling. I want to send good messages and meanings along the way. The journey is about spreading love and understanding. Not using each other. Not distraction. Tools for presence in life. I want to bond with like-minded people who echo my appreciation and awareness for them. It's hard making friends when everyone sees you as something useful to them. I want partners, not products. I'm just protective. I don't think I work well in groups. This is all so weird. It's my name and my life . . . but I'm selling it? Is that what I'm doing? I hope that's not what I'm doing. I have no idea what I'm doing.

In 2012 I was navigating ambition and isolation.

I'd always had a close group of friends growing up. Emotional support, financial support, you name it, we were there for each other.

But I had a cardinal rule about group projects: I didn't do them. I don't work well in groups because I'm insecure about my own abilities and I don't want to drag anybody down. I had always kept friendship and work separate, and it was all good.

Then I arrived in Los Angeles, a town that functions on nepotism: to survive, you had to believe that your ideas were better than everyone else's ideas, and you had to rely on an inner circle of people who could help you make things happen. But I didn't have an inner circle in LA yet, and the people around me were encouraging me to change my ideas to fit into theirs. Not to mention the constant pressure to "strike while the iron is hot"[4] because time was running out and opportunities were fleeting. It was being hammered into my head from all sides that I had one chance to turn my small screens into a bigger project, which felt to me like my one chance to make a *big* mistake. I was being told that my online success with *My Drunk Kitchen* was a fluke and that if I didn't move on it NOW I was a failure. And I believed it.

(Additionally, LA was super hot. Which I hate. Bleh.)

All I wanted was time and space, a private learning curve to make mistakes and process them. However, it didn't feel as though that was an option. I had moved out to LA and taken another big risk, and who was I to ruminate about it? But I couldn't help myself. When I get scared, my instincts aren't fight or flight; I just want to lie on the floor and stare up at the ceiling.

Fortunately in those foggy months I was blessed to be living with some really good people. My roommates, Pearl and Hillary, were incredibly kind as I adjusted to LA life and asked questions that I realize now must have been incredibly amateur. We met through a producer I had dinner with who was moving out of her place and into one with

---

4 I like to say "Make the iron hot by continually striking."

her boyfriend. The apartment had three bedrooms, and I moved into the one she had recently vacated. They introduced me to their group of friends, who had all met at Emerson College, a talented group with a passion for media and experience in the realities of "the biz." I often felt sort of embarrassed to be getting all these meetings and all this attention for my channel when I had no idea what I was doing and they were all working so hard. I felt as though I didn't deserve any of it. I was carrying around a lot of shame about the value of my work, especially in a space where there were *so many* deserving stories that should be shared.[5]

Outside of that group, trying to meet people was tough. I found myself being scoffed at across tables in bars by independent filmmakers who would lean in close to my face and ask in a slow, drunken slur why the Internet was ruining art. I wanted to reply, "I'm not trying to ruin art! I'm trying to build a small business." But instead I would just sip my drink and slink away. Slink. Drink. Repeat. That was 2012 for me.

Things started to get a little better when fellow up-and-coming Internet kid Grace Helbig moved to LA. We had met in New York, and I had seen her do improv. It was awesome. She rocked. And she was one of the hardest-working people I had ever met. She came from a traditional entertainment background so she understood how to straddle the two worlds of old and new media. She helped me to deal with my disillusionment about the entertainment industry. She explained to me how things worked in a way that didn't make me feel inadequate.

Professional life aside, I was still processing personal life as well, trying to shake off the last of my latent homophobic tensions. I actually remember a lesbian asking me at some point that year, "Oh no, you're

---

5   Spoiler alert: The Internet creates a space for that!! Hurray!!

not one of those self-hating gays, are you?" And it stung because . . . well, I totally was.

So by the end of 2012, I was exhausted, depleted, and desperate to leave Hollywood to regain a sense of who I was. Maybe I could still get a real job back in New York. There weren't *that* many videos of me drunk on the Internet. I could get a job at Google! Or work in social media! I loved apps and tech stuff . . . that could be a nice life.

But when I thought about giving up on YouTube, I knew I would miss my connection with my 400K subscriber community. A connection that had formed for almost two years. When I first started making videos, I got a public PO box and would periodically get letters from people who felt I was someone they could open up to, or who just wanted to put some thoughts down on paper and send them my way. I would write back to everyone and seal it with a cute little H-shaped wax stamp, thanking them for watching and offering my own thoughts and advice if they asked me for it. It all felt very manageable and small and safe. However, the more discouraged I got about my time in LA, the less I felt able to reply. How could I offer those people guidance on their lives when I so clearly didn't know what I was doing with my own?

Not only that . . . but these people thought they knew me, but none of them knew that I was gay. And was that something I was hiding? I couldn't be sure.

Earlier that year, Anderson Cooper came out. It was a big deal. Everybody talked about it for months and months. People questioned why he had stayed in the closet for so long and frankly . . . I kind of felt bad for him. I didn't think it was something that people had the right to judge or question. At the same time, as a silent member of the LGBT+ community, I felt connected to him in a way I hadn't before. And I wondered if I was denying myself that same connection.

So before leaving the public eye completely, I wanted to make something to make sure I moved past that "self-hating gay" phase. I wanted to be out and proud. So I posted a coming-out video on You-Tube. Nine unedited minutes of me awkwardly trying to condense my journey into video form.

The influx of support and compassion from my community was unbelievably re-invigorating.[6] I felt encouraged and inspired and energized and free. It didn't matter what the people of the city of Los Angeles believed about my career choices or my mistakes or even my triumphs. What mattered was that I was sharing a version of myself that was authentic, making entertainment for a group of people that understood me. Feeling like we understood each other. They were my company in the Kitchen in the House Party of Life. They were the ones I was cooking for.

After that coming-out video I was able to finally sell that cookbook I'd been dreaming of and I had more confidence about my sense of purpose and accountability. I decided to launch a crowd-funded tour across the country to meet the people who'd made my journey possible. A tour that launched at $50K but eventually received $220K of support. A tour that was originally slated for ten cities but grew into twenty-two. A tour that actually left me a little bit in the red financially but rich beyond my wildest dreams emotionally.

My roommate Pearl was the one who made it happen. Through Pearl's diligence and hard work we were able to run a campaign and

---

6 There is one e-mail I often reference when talking about what changed after the coming-out video. It came from a dad in Nebraska who told me that he and his family had watched videos on my channel not knowing that I was gay—and that they hadn't approved of homosexuality in the past, but now I'd given them something to think about.

launch a tour that would have three elements in each city where we stopped: an episode of *My Drunk Kitchen* shot in the home of someone who'd donated; an episode of *Hello, Harto!*, a mockumentary style show documenting our attempts to make a show on the road; and a "live event."

The "live event" was the thing we couldn't quite get a grip on. Until a conversation that went something like this:

HANNAH: "We should do something nice at meetups. Like a donation drive."

PEARL: "Why don't we host the meetups at food banks?"

HANNAH: "OH, MY GOD, AND WE CAN ALL VOLUNTEER TO-GETHER!"

PEARL: "THAT WOULD BE AWESOME! A WAY OF GIVING BACK TO THE LOCAL COMMUNITY!!"

HANNAH: "IT WILL FEEL SO GOOD FOR THE SOUL!!!!"

Then I'm pretty sure we high-fived and hugged a bunch.

So the tour began, and not only did we film an episode of *Kitchen* and an episode of *Hello, Harto!* in each city, but we also hosted events at local food banks, encouraging people to join us for three to four hours of volunteering. We called this piece of the tour "Have a Hart Day"!

Visiting food banks while on the road gave us a bird's-eye view of the different food resources available in each of the twenty-two cities. For instance, Second Harvest Food Bank in Oregon makes its own almond butter for distribution. Whereas at the food bank in Detroit, volunteers spent the day chipping frozen meat out of giant blocks of ice. It was a fascinating (and sometimes devastating) view of America. Or rather, a view of the many different "Americas" that exist in our shared land.

The tour was both exhausting and exhilarating. We hit high-

highs (Board & Brew, I'm lookin' at you!) and low-lows (Toronto, I know I had a fever and flu and should forgive myself, but I will forever be sorry that I called you Portland), and it was worth every moment. We[7] traveled the country in an RV and all worked ourselves into the ground. I got to meet and hug so many cool and impressive people, from a low-income defense lawyer helping survivors of domestic violence to SparkFun, a company dedicated to making at-home electronics projects possible, to a woman working with special-needs adolescents who was hurled across the room (she was okay!) by one of her clients to a teenager who was struggling to overcome self-harm and taking the steps to get there. Old people, young people, LGBTQA+++++ people, straight people, all sorts of people came out to volunteer with us. It was sweaty work, and sometimes I would be tired, but by the end of the day I was always restored by the positivity of those around me.

And the best part? Even after the tour ended, "Have a Hart Day" kept going strong. Today we even have membership cards!

---

7   Pearl as producer, our friend Sam as director, and Pearl's boyfriend, Nick, as the driver.

At this point, there have been "Have a Hart Day" volunteer events in fifteen different countries: Australia, Singapore, Canada, Germany, Mexico, New Zealand, Brazil, England, Wales, Netherlands, Sweden, Malaysia, Philippines, Scotland, and in cities across the United States! Shout out to all our awesome City Captains![8]

I'm so proud of "Have a Hart Day" and what it accomplishes. I love seeing the kinship that forms between volunteers and the relief that is found in spending a day thinking of things other than yourself. Sometimes it's the only thing that comforts me on dark days when my brain is in a downward spiral of negativity. What makes me especially happy is that it's not something *I* did. It's something *we* did. It's the biggest group project I've ever participated in, and I couldn't be happier.

When I used to think back on 2012, and picture my confused, sweaty self trying to figure things out in LA, I would view it as a failed year. But failure and success are not so simply defined. That year may have been a failure in terms of tangible career growth, but the self-knowledge and acceptance was the success. Every time I stood up for myself, that was a success. Every time I realized my

---

8   Check out have-a-hart-day.tumblr.com for more info.

limitations, that was a success. It wasn't a year of external gain, but of internal growth.

Now when I think about it, I realize that without the events of 2012, I would never have launched the tour in 2013.

Milton says, "The mind can make a heaven of hell, or a hell of heaven." I try remind myself daily that success and failure have less to do with actual results but rather how we choose to respond to the results. You can squander success and you can overcome failure. You can flourish or you can flounder. Sometimes it's about choosing which feelings to fight and which feelings to follow.

THAT SUMMER FEELING

It's 3 p.m. on a Sunday, and I'm sitting with my laptop in a café near my house. This is the first time I've left the house all day because today the fog is winning.

The fog is what I call my depressive downswings. If you're someone who also has "major depressive disorder," you know what the fog can feel like. If you don't, I'll try to describe it below.

Depression feels like:

* A low hum in your head, just loud enough to make you aware of it but not loud enough for you to act out against it. It gets louder when you move toward things you normally enjoy (friends, family, coffee, work, movement) but don't any longer. Which is why you then find yourself walking toward the couch and lying down to stare at the ceiling.

* A lead fog that surrounds you, obscuring your vision only slightly but making every movement ten times harder. It's at its thickest when you get back into bed in the middle of the day. You could reward yourself for getting up in

the first place, but now that you're back in bed you know you've failed, so why celebrate at all?

* A wordless whisperer telling you that *this* feeling is the true feeling and that every other feeling you've had was only temporary. This is your lasting reality. Those moments you called happiness or peace were just distraction, but this is you at your most real. Don't bother to fight against it, because you're always fighting against it, and since you're fighting against your own nature, you'll never fully win.

Depression is the evangelist for emptiness.

For me, compassion and companionship are the enemies of depression, the best ways to fight it. Compassion for myself because I know I'm struggling. Companionship because I can't fight it alone.

I started taking my depression seriously earlier this year. As a result, I'm learning about things I can do to combat it, I'm also learning to identify my triggers. Loneliness feeds my downswings. That and the heat. For me the feeling of depression is sticky and sweltering. Like a hot summer air that makes it hard to breathe. That's why long before I knew what depression was, I just called those low moods and moments "that summer feeling."

Sometimes I have to reassure myself that I am real.

Summertime was the most dreaded time of the year for me as a kid. Like most children of single mothers, we were left home alone a lot. My earliest memories of being home alone start in the summer after first grade. But those early years were better because Naomi was around and she would dig holes with me in the backyard and we would take mud baths. Once when we were digging, we found a rusted antique toy race car. Mom said it was from the 1920s and it was true treasure. I wish I still had that race car. Those times playing together in the backyard are some of my happiest memories. We'd pretend that we were on "away missions" like the characters from *Star Trek*. Naomi was three years older and braver, and she would show me how to pick lemons and loquats off the trees to eat. Once we ate some lemons when they were still green (Naomi told me that green lemons were okay to eat because they were called "limes") and had terrible diarrhea afterward. Still a happy memory though.

Then Naomi got to the age of sleepovers and trips with friends' families, and I was left to spend those long summer days in our house by myself, trying to get the TV antenna to pick up anything I could watch. Our TV was from a thrift store, and some of the buttons had fallen off the front (to be honest, I may have been the one who had broken them off), and so to channel surf I'd have to stick my finger through the slot to poke the small black disk that connected the wires to change the station. We only got two channels more often than not, 2 and 44, and I'd spend my time clicking through all forty-two channels of static to be sure that nothing had changed. I watched so much daytime television and so many reruns that I had memorized the character arcs and even the commercials.

I got good at staying still when I was alone because I had injured myself too many times already when I didn't. Once I lit a match and put it back into the matchbox with the other matches, which instantly caught on fire. I was so startled that I threw the box into the fireplace, and the fire grew. I started adding the trash from the floor to the fire, and it continued to grow. I thought my mom would be proud when she came home to find that the trash was gone and that I had cleaned up. Unfortunately, some of the old envelopes I had thrown into the flames were important. It was hard to tell what was mail and what was junk in our house. Everything was covered in coffee stains. My mother didn't yell, though I could tell she was angry and I'd done a bad thing. I didn't play with matches again, which was fine, but it chipped away at my already limited entertainment options.

I slept on the couch a lot. I was hungry a lot. I was bored a lot. I traced the outline of the Chinese chest[1] with my fingertips and imagined what every person in the village was doing, and wondered if the shapes of the trees on it were real trees because I had never seen trees like that. Sometimes I would do arts and crafts. My favorite was to collect ash from all the ashtrays around the house and spit into it to make a paste and give myself tattoos. Another arts and crafts activity I did was carving "H" into the desk or floor. I hid from the mailman. I never opened the door for strangers or answered the phone. I was a good little latchkey child.

I spent much of the day peeking through the sheets on the windows (who needs curtains, when you've got sheets!), looking for any sign that someone was coming home. Once I woke to find my

---

1   As I've mentioned my mother wasn't very good with money. Our power would go off and the water wouldn't work, but she did bring home wonderful things from "garage sailing" like the Chinese chest, a massive, ornate, solid piece of furniture with a village scene carved into the front.

mother's green coat on the couch, and I was overjoyed because it meant she hadn't left for work yet. She rarely changed outfits, and she absolutely never left without that coat. I ran through the house looking for her, but I couldn't find her. That was okay, though, because she had probably just run out for a minute and would be coming back soon. Maybe she'd gone out to get donuts and we were going to have breakfast together! That pink box!

I decided to surprise her, and I hid under the coat on the couch. I was giggling and giddy because she would definitely laugh when she grabbed the coat and found me underneath. Then she'd say that since she was already late for work, she might as well just stay home with me. Or maybe I could go with her. I could sit under her desk while she transcribed audio from newscasts. It was going to be a wonderful day.

I don't know how long I waited under that coat. I think I fell asleep, because suddenly the sun was much higher in the sky and the house had heated up substantially. Our house had many windows, so it would get very warm and sleepy inside.

Eventually I crawled out from under the coat and walked to the bathroom. I took off my shirt, wet it in the bathtub, and put it back on to cool off. I drank some water from the bathtub faucet—bathtub water was the cleanest; the kitchen sink was off limits since it was always clogged—and walked back to the couch.

Before resuming my place under the coat for what was still sure to be a wonderful prank, I peeked out the window just in case she was about to walk up. There were men outside talking by the car repair place across the street. The sweat was sticking their shirts to their backs in different patterns. It was like looking at clouds, trying to make out which shapes looked like faces, like animals, and so on. I wondered if their sweat made their shirts cooler, as the bathtub water had made mine. Everyone seemed to be hot that day.

Then suddenly it clicked.

It was hot outside. And no one would need a coat on such a hot day.

That is my first memory of feeling a deep self-disgust. I felt disappointed, but I also felt stupid. My hope had broken my own heart, all because I didn't think it through. I wept into the coat and used it like a pillow. I wanted to fall asleep. I wanted time to pass. I wasn't just bored. I was lonely.

By the time third grade rolled around, my mother had started dating her boss. That man would eventually become her second husband and Maggie's father. His name was David, and he moved in with us that year, and when summer came his son, who I'll call Matthew, came to visit. Matthew had a fat nose like a pug and a sandy blond bowl cut. He was older than Naomi, already a teenager, pockmarked and greasy. His eyes were blue and beady. He liked comic books and was able to do all sorts of things because he was a boy that I couldn't do because I was a girl and that was just the way things were.

That summer Matthew became my regular companion. Unfortunately, he had a bit of an affinity for violence. He once showed me a scary comic called *Spawn*. One issue featured an alcoholic father who came home every night to beat his wife and children. I was horrified. Our household wasn't the cleanest or the most "normal," but it was never a violent home. Matthew told me that if I was scared of violence, it was only because I didn't know how to defend myself. So he decided it was up to him to teach me self-defense. But when we started our self-defense lessons, it was clear

Matthew and I weren't evenly matched. After all, he was five years older than me.

One day, Matthew said he was going to teach me how to escape a chokehold. I told Matthew that I didn't want to learn that one, and he chased me down the hall to the front door. I'd been trained never to open the front door, so once I reached it I turned to face him and he choked me, lifting me off the ground until I was on the tips of my toes. I kicked him as hard as I could in the stomach and crotch, and he sputtered and stopped.

Naomi came home (or appeared from another room) and was upset and told Matthew to stop. He said we were playing pro wrestling and lifted me and slammed me on his knee. The wind was knocked out of me, my back hurt, and I couldn't really move. Naomi called our mom and told her that she needed to come home from work right away to take me to the hospital. I was angry at Naomi for doing that because Mom had lost a job before for having to take me to the hospital (the incident with the knife). I felt responsible for what had happened. If I'd known how to defend myself better she wouldn't have had to leave work.

Mom came home and we went to the ER, and the doctor was annoyed and sent us home because my back was only bruised and not broken. I was embarrassed and felt guilty for pulling Mom out of work and wasting everyone's time. But it was Naomi's fault, too. She was always interfering.

The next day Mom and David made Matthew go to work with them, and Naomi was off somewhere else, and I was home alone again. The emptiness of the house felt magnified somehow. I was hot and sad, and I felt as though my head was filled with cotton. I didn't open the windows when I was home alone because Mom had told us once about a kid who was napping by a window when a kidnapper reached through and snatched him out. I felt guilty. "As a family" it was decided that Matthew wasn't allowed to be alone with me anymore, which was supposed to be a good thing, but being left in my silent solitude again, I felt punished.

It wasn't fair. Why should I be punished for being too weak to be left alone with Matthew? Maybe it was a sign that I needed to strike out on my own.

I packed all of my belongings onto a stick just like "hobos" did in cartoons. I took my boogie rag[2] and laid it on the floor and tried to think of what to pack. I didn't want to take anything that Naomi might want, and there wasn't much food in the cupboards, so my options were scarce. What I did find was a pie crust in a pie tin and some Jell-O packets. I laid those on the rag and looked for something to tie the rag around. I pulled the rubber head off the plunger and used the handle.

I left a note for my mother and sister using some binder paper and a pencil I sharpened with a knife. I added the knife to my pack. I wrote that I was sure they wouldn't miss me and that I loved them very much, but that this was the best thing for me to do. I told David that I would miss him, too. The only one I didn't mention in the note was Matthew, hoping to hurt his feelings. I was an emotional mastermind.

As I left the house, I turned back and waved good-bye to the people inside. That was a habit. Whenever I left the house during the school year, I would pretend to say good-bye to people who weren't there, just in case someone was watching and tracking my move-

---

2   We were often out of toilet paper, so every time we got sick we'd use our baby blankets, which we then called "boogie rags" and carried around to snot into. It was a great way to save paper! We were going green!

ments. My mom told me that our neighborhood had "prowlers" who would hide behind fences and watch for empty houses.

I crossed the dead grass and patchy dirt of our front lawn and headed in the direction of the nearest park. In my new life on my own I was going to do whatever I wanted, and I wanted to make some friends. There were always kids at the park with their families and with summer camps. I could make some fast friends and maybe even get a snack out of it later that afternoon. Hell, maybe even a juice box! Luxury.

Another benefit of going to the park was that by the time night began to fall I could set myself up behind some bushes. I would sleep in the park and then head for the train station in the morning. Then, because I was a kid, I would just get on the train with a group of adults and no one would be the wiser. (Clearly my plan had many holes, but at the time it seemed flawless. I even thought that I could make friends with a monkey and we would entertain people for money. Legit.)

As I walked toward the park, I did a lap around my school to see if there was anything left on the playground that could be of some use to me in my new life. But the gates were all locked because school was out of session. I continued my way parkward and was about to cross the street alone for the very first time. I was becoming an independent adult already![3]

"Hey there!"

Before I could cross, a truck pulled up in front of me and a man shouted through his passenger window, "Do you live around here?"

---

3 We lived on the same block as my elementary school, so even though the journey felt very long and far, I hadn't traveled even a block from my house.

Stranger danger. I felt my feet freeze to the ground. Without my consent, my head nodded.

"Do you know how to get to Howard Street?"

My heart was beating hard in my chest. I was so scared of that man and his truck. I felt the hairs stand up on my arms. They were scared of him, too. I shook my head no.

"Are you sure? I thought it was right around here."

I was lying. Howard Street was only two blocks from where we were. Maybe I was being paranoid. I thought of my father. He would be ashamed to see me lying to someone. I shouldn't lie. Lying is sinning. Sinning is wrong. God hates sinners, and I don't want God to hate me. I spoke and pointed. "It's that way."

"Which way?"

I pointed harder. "That way."

"Listen." He leaned across his seat and opened his car door. "It's close, right? Wanna just get in and show me? That would be a big help."

I thought of my mother. She had taught us to follow our feelings and that our feelings came from God and trusting God was trusting your gut. She said if you ever feel afraid, just start screaming and don't stop. But I was torn between the conflicting teachings of my parents, so instead I just said "No" and backed toward the school.

His smile cracked, and behind his eyes I could see anger.

"Bitch."

He peeled out from the curb with his door slamming shut in the process. I ran back to my house as fast as I could.

Once I was back inside, I felt such comfort in the familiar feeling of home. I couldn't run away. I was a child. The world was big and bad. Both of my parents could agree on that even if they couldn't agree with each other. I would be in such danger out there on my own.

So I had to choose between feeling lonely and feeling scared. Loneliness I knew. Feeling scared was foreign. I looked at my letter, tore it up, and never told my family about my attempt to run away. Night time would come and the house would be full again soon enough.

Shortly thereafter, Matthew was taken to a group home for juvenile delinquents after he'd gotten in some big trouble at school. My mom said that he'd been wrongly declared "mentally ill" and insisted that "mental illness" was made up by "garbage-sucking scum buckets." She had taught us that all medications were evil and to be wary of doctors because they wanted to tear our family apart and drug us and stick us in hospitals.

I think it was after that summer that I began to look at my mother differently. After the incidents with Matthew and seeing that she still had affection for him, I started to question not only her judgment but also her thinking. I knew she loved me, but why didn't she see the need to protect me? Weren't all children worth protecting?

As children, we think that whatever world surrounds us is normal. As I entered fourth and fifth grades and began spending time in the homes of other kids, my world grew. I spent a lot of time watching and thinking about the way people interacted with other people. I began to see that not all families were like mine. I realized that healthy relationships weren't born out of the desperation to avoid a feeling of loneliness. And that loneliness can come with you into even the most crowded of rooms.

These days I'm learning to value my solitude. Turns out I'm a bit of an introvert. I haven't been magically cured of my depressive tendencies but I am learning to manage them better. One of the most important things I've learned is that the mind is like a muscle and it can be trained (or in some cases retrained) with time, energy, attention, and care and through meditation, medication, and sometimes even simple conversation. I think of it as being like training for a marathon: you have to put in the time and the effort to see results and there will be good days and bad days, but you will move forward as long as you move through them all.

The day I tried to run away was scary, but I did take something positive away from it. After that day I started to walk around the neighborhood more often. It was a great way to pass the time, and I had learned I could trust myself to stay safe and avoid danger. And now, in my adult life, I make it a practice to walk for at least thirty minutes every day. It helps get me out of the house and out of my head.

I also have a visual reminder: a print of Little Red Riding Hood walking through the woods with the wolf.

For me, dealing with depression isn't about trying to run away from the feeling; it's about learning to walk alongside it.

FEAR AND ECSTASY

I used to like drugs more than I do now. I went through a period after college when I was living in San Francisco and stuck in a rut. It's not that things were all bad, but I was living in that post-college state, still partying and drinking like I was a student, and it started to wear on me. At the time I was sharing an apartment with one of my best friends, Hannah Gelb, and her boyfriend, Alex. I considered myself bisexual then, but only to mask the crushes I had on Hannah's friends from UC Santa Cruz.[1] Over time, our wild nights of drinking and spontaneous dance parties weren't enough to keep me going. Life was just . . . still. And everything seemed to come with a caveat. I had graduated from college, but the job market was tanking. I was comfortable being gay-ish, I guess, but I was always hanging out with my straight friends, who were all in relationships, and was nowhere close to finding a partner of my own. We had Mom off the

---

1   Julianne, Maria, if you guys are reading this book, well, the truth is that I
    was always trying to make out with one of you. Maybe both of you?

streets for the moment, but without medication and treatment she would only get worse; we had put a Band-Aid over something that was starting to fester. I felt as if I were trapped in a holding pattern.

Then I went to a party and decided to try coke.

The effects were not what I expected—more like an incredibly strong cup of coffee than any sort of druggy delirium. Coke just made everything seem interesting again. However, I quickly realized if I needed to do a key bump in the bathroom of El Rio while my friends sang karaoke outside with KJ Paul[2] in order to stay positive and have a good time . . . well, then, clearly I wasn't really having a good time. And if I could no longer have a good time participating in my favorite sport,[3] there had to be something wrong in my head and my heart. So I accepted the truth and announced to my friends that I was getting seriously stagnant in San Francisco and needed something more out of life. Aside from the semester I'd spent in Japan during college, my entire existence had taken place within a twenty-mile radius of San Francisco. Staying close to home wasn't helping me break old patterns of caretaking behavior with my mom or making her any better (and I could help pay her bills from anywhere). I wasn't challenging myself to chart new waters. I was just wading in still ones.

At the time I was working two jobs: during the day I worked as a property manager for a small-business owner who lived in Noe Valley but who was mostly on perma-vacation in Cabo, and at night I would head to my job as a part-time proofreader for Geotext Translations. I really liked that job. It was like white-collar mining, hunt-

---

2   KJ Paul is a karaoke jockey. Yes, this is a real and awesome thing. He ruled.
3   I love karaoke more than any other sport. And karaoke is a sport, by the way. Makes you sweaty, increases your heart rate, pumps you full of endorphins. If that's not a sport, then I don't know what is.

ing for errors in stacks of paper until 11 p.m., when I would catch the Muni home. Geotext had offices all over the world, in San Francisco, New York, London, Tokyo, Singapore, and I think also in Hong Kong. I heard about a part-time position opening up in NYC and decided to go for it. And I got the job! So I drained my savings and moved to New York to sleep on couches and gain a bunch of weight and eventually make the first episode of *My Drunk Kitchen* as a way of trying to cheer up Hannah Gelb.

I had moved to New York to get myself in gear and to start out fresh in a new city. Little did I know that the move would lead me someplace totally unexpected: to the middle of the desert for Burning Man.

NOTES FROM BURNING MAN—DAY ONE

Don't listen to him, he's got a "backie"—that's a person you've always got on the back of your mind.

Not much negativity, though I feel like everyone has this weird reverse passive aggressive thing going on.

Out of the 60K people who arrived . . . How many full sets of golf clubs are here?

Grilled Cheese Camp

Burning MANtality—it's a mix between camping and a rave

Burning Man is just a way for people to convince you to take your clothes off.

I went to Burning Man in the summer of 2011. I had been invited to go as the guest of a frequent Burner who worked at YouTube's corporate office. He reached out and told me that he thought I would have a great time and that it would be an awesome place to make an episode of *My Drunk Kitchen*. This would only be the twelfth episode of the "show," but I was already scrambling for concepts. Burning Man started in 1986 (Just like me! #twinning!) and can be described as the world's biggest pop-up event. But it's a lot more than that. It's really a sudden city in the desert where everyone gets in touch with their bodies, their minds, and their spiritual sides—and these days they get to try out new apps there, too. Burning Man has changed, man.

Before accepting the invitation I called my soul sister Morgan and asked her for advice on whether it was safe to go. Morgan has been in my life for as long as my biological sister Naomi has. They actually met first, when they were both two years old. Morgan had been to Burning Man before and knew all the right questions to ask, like how well I knew this guy and whether I trusted him. I told her that he worked for YouTube, was older and married with kids, and his wife would be there, too. He seemed like a techy dork who just wanted to get high in the desert. I wasn't worried. After that, her main concern was whether I could afford the trip, because going to Burning Man had become increasingly expensive over the years. I reassured her that my ticket and transport into the camp were covered and that all I had to do was fly myself to Reno and back. She also asked about my plans for bringing water,[4] and I told her that I would be in an experienced camp of Burners, some of whom had been attending since the very first festival, and that they were going to take care of everything for me, including all my water, my gear, and even my food. "You totally lucked out!" she said. "Go and have a great time."

I landed in the Reno airport, and when I saw people in massive fur coats holding glow sticks, I knew I was heading in the right direction. I took a smaller plane and then a jeep to the camp itself. When I arrived it was still early in the setup. At Burning Man there are four days of build (when everyone builds their massive statues or experiences or pillow forts or whatever) and then four days of burn. Or maybe it's six days of build and two days of burn? Or four days of build, two days of burn, and two days of afterburn? I don't really remember. Regardless, I planned to spend three nights there. I was nervous about traveling solo, and that much time in the desert with strangers seemed like plenty.

There was no cell service anywhere, so I had to just kind of navigate my way toward my friends by asking people. I found them pretty

---

4   A person needs to bring 1.5 gallons of water per day to Burning Man.

easily because it was still early in the build stages and people were just kind of milling around, waiting for the rest of the city folk to arrive.

The first day and night I didn't partake in much. No booze, no smoke, no nada. I just wanted to get the lay of the land and gauge the people I was camping with. I wanted to take in the experience with my senses unencumbered. Initial observations included: *lots of white people, lots of dust, lots of butts, lots of boobies, hard to sleep without earplugs.* I wanted to ease in at my own pace, so I kept to myself. I was probably a bit of a bummer burner, but that was fine by me. We all need to process at our own speed.

I slept in a pup tent in our camp, and everyone was pretty respectful of my hesitance to join in. Nobody was in a rush, it seemed, and since supplies in camp were limited, whatever goodies I didn't want just meant more for everybody else. I didn't start to relax and let my guard down until the morning of the second day, when I woke and took a walk by myself around the camps. It was dawn, and I watched the landscape around me change from red to pink to white.[5] Burning Man takes place in the Black Rock Desert on the dried-up prehistoric lake bed of Lake Lahontan, which everyone calls the playa. The ground is cracked and covered in an incredibly fine silt. According to the Burning Man website, the silt has a high-alkaline pH, which makes it incredibly corrosive. That, in combination with the sudden windstorms, means that dust gets into just about everything. A fair amount embedded itself in my bones, I'm pretty sure.

As I wandered the various camps, I saw people on bikes and people making food and people doing yoga and people being tied to a wooden post and whipped in a BDSM camp. There were many things to observe. I kept my head down for the most part, not talk-

---

5   That's the reverse order of my terrible sunburn.

ing to anyone and jotting down random sentences in my journal in hopes of turning them into jokes I could use to film *My Drunk Kitchen* the next day:[6]

OVERHEARD ON DAY TWO—
BURN WORLD PROBLEMS:

* *"REI has really gone downhill."*

* *"Dropped my headlamp in the port o' potty, but the batteries are still good."*

* *"Meet us between the giant beating heart and the Cheshire cat playing dubstep."*

* *"A shame they don't sell the Costco carport anymore."*

* *"When you get nervous, picture everybody nakcd. Oh wait, they already are."*

As I walked back to camp, the dawn coolness had worn off and the temperature was rising fast. I was a little lost and decided to retrace my steps using landmarks. I wasn't really nervous, but I was becoming hot and uncomfortable. Anyone who knows me is well aware that I am an absolute water fiend. I'm almost oppressive in my need for hydration. I want everyone to drink as much water as I do all the time.

But like a big ol' dumb-dumb I had forgotten my water bottle. It happens. Nobody is perfect.

---

6   Check it out if you get the chance: YouTube.com/Harto. :D

I passed a camp with a water tank and decided to be brave and ask if I could have some. Everyone around me seemed comfortable sharing with strangers, so maybe I could be comfortable, too. I walked up to the group, all sitting on rugs on the ground looking like they were born to burn, and asked quietly if I could have some of their water, half hoping that no one would hear me.

Unfortunately, I was noticed right away, and someone said that I was more than welcome to have some of their water, but did I have a cup? Of course I didn't. I had left my Nalgene in my tent like a double dumb-dumb. So I just stood there, distracted and dehydrated and now wanting desperately to find my way back. Someone else in the group eventually took pity on me and asked if I had anything I could trade for one of their cups. I blanked. I had my black journal and my pen, but I didn't feel like I could part with either. I also had my goggles and my bandana (which I used to wipe the goggles and wrap around my face to protect from sudden sandstorms), but my companions back at camp had told me that those were the only things I shouldn't really trade. Plus they were borrowed.

I stared at them, and they stared back at me while I thought.

Burning Man functioned (and functioned well!) on a barter system. There was no money, but you could trade goods for goods or goods for services or services for goods. I couldn't trade any of the goods I had in my possession . . . but maybe I could trade a service? I tried to think of things I was good at. I'm good at giving massages,[7] but giving massages to the sweaty and semi-stoned seemed like a little too much too fast. There was something else I was good at, but it seemed kind of lame. But it was that or nothing.

---

7 Like really, really good. Wink.

"I have a pen and some paper. I could . . . write you some puns? Or a poem? Or both?"

I was grateful then for the heat so they couldn't see my face turn bright red. Suddenly there was laughter, and with laughter came relief.

"Yeah, that's awesome, you can have my cup. Can you write me something about a turtle?"

The guy who asked wore a wooden turtle around his neck, and I wrote him a poem about being a turtle safe in its shell but never getting to see the world. Or something like that. I wish that I had made a copy, but at the time I was so excited about accomplishing my goal that I just ripped it out of my journal and handed it to him. He thanked me, and they offered me drugs or booze free of charge, but I just took my cup, saying that water was fine, thank you. The Playa provides.

I returned to camp excited to tell everyone about what I had done. I was elated. I had taken care of myself as a stranger in a strange land, and I was ready for whatever came next. I felt like I belonged.

Naturally, that meant that I was ready to party.

My last night at Burning Man was the first night of "The Burn," which is when all the burning of the wooden idols happens. Sounds pretty pagan, right? It is. Or at least its roots were very earthy and spiritual. Actually, watching it all unfold is sort of like watching a bunch of Bay Area artists and tech people gathered together in the middle of the desert to forsake their clothing and their privileges (and in some cases their marriages), in the hope of connecting with something—something greater, something smaller, just connecting with something, anything again. I know that's what it was about for me. Aside from the marriage-forsaking part. I definitely wasn't married. Still not married!

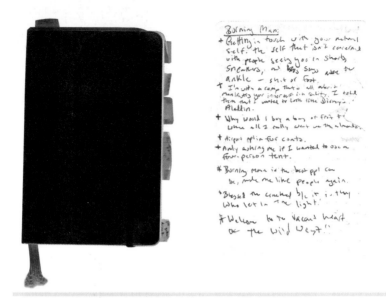

BURNING MAN—DAY THREE

* *Getting in touch with your natural self. The self that isn't concerned with people seeing you in shorts, sneakers, and socks above the ankle.*

* *I'm with a camp that is all about manifesting your inner self into reality. I told them that I wanted to look like Disney's Aladdin.*

* *Someone asked me if I wanted to sleep in a four-person tent.*

* *"Burning man is the best ppl can be, made me like people again"—old white military dude*

* *"blessed be the cracked, because they are those who let in light"—people crying camp*

* *"Welcome to the vacant heart of the Wild West."*

Where was I? Oh yes. It was the last night at Burning Man, and I was about to take MDMA, otherwise known as Ecstasy, for the first and only time. Oh wait, I'm skipping ahead.

At that point I had drunk the Kool-Aid and was in full Burning Man mode. I had changed my name (to something sacred that could not be written down for the human eye to see but only be spoken for the human heart to hear[8]) and had my arms painted blue with "tribal"[9] symbols. I wore the same white tank top I had arrived in and had borrowed some Aladdin pants from a costume camp that made me feel like a god.

So when a cute little lady wandered into our camp to make friends with my Burner family and then pulled out a capsule that looked like a dirty vitamin, I was happy to let the good times roll. And roll they did.

Before I go any further, I'd like to inform you, gentle reader, that I was a nervous nelly about taking this drug. I asked a bunch of questions, including who in our group *wasn't* going to be taking drugs and whether there were safety precautions in place in case anything went wrong and what the effects of the drugs were going to be. My CAMPanions[10] were patient and parental and soothing. They told me it would make me feel relaxed and happy and awake but not agitated. *Everything will just feel more beautiful.* The effects would last only long enough to round out the night. And that I shouldn't mix anything with it since it was my first time. I felt young and inexperienced but also free and reckless—a novel combination for me.

---

8 AKA I forgot what the name was.

9 Forgive me! I was young! And foolish! And appropriating culture!

10 Like "Camp" = "Companion"! Also I JUST CAME UP WITH THAT AND FEEL SO PROUD OF MYSELF!

The Girl Who Wandered Over[11] told me that the only real danger would be the comedown,[12] and then I'd have to ask myself whether or not I wanted to keep rolling.

"How will I know when I'm coming down?"

"When all the judgment starts to seep back in."

A night free from my judgment of myself and those around me? Sign me the fuck up.

So I drank some tea and took the drug and left my notebook in my tent.

As darkness fell, I kept asking myself whether I was feeling any-thing. I wanted to pinpoint the exact moment when the drug took effect. But the actual change was subtle, and I never really felt as if a big shift was happening. I just knew I was having an amazing time. A blissful and relaxing walk through the dusk. I stared at the ground and at my feet. Every step I took looked like a breath as the dust puffed up around my shoes. I loved those shoes. They did such a good job of keeping my feet safe. Shoes were really wonderful when you stopped and thought about it. Were any of the others thinking the same thing about their shoes? Someone had lights on theirs! I bent down to ex-amine the lights rubbing at the dust to see if there was more light to reveal. There was. It looked magnificent. I had to tell the wearer.

"Your shoes are magnificent."

The person laughed. "Thanks, brother."

Wait. Who was this person? One of my friends? Who knew? Where were my friends? Oh there they were!

---

11 Who needs names?
12 For the real comedown, see the chapter "Casual Travel Asshole."

"Thank you for being so kind to me." I hugged the Girl Who Wandered Over. She was magnificent, too.

She smiled and put both hands against my face. Her eyes were filled with light. My friends (*they were my friends!*) were so sweet to me. And this girl, who had been a stranger an hour before, was now someone I *knew* I could trust. We all trust until we're taught otherwise. I reached out to stroke the fur of her jacket, and *it was so soft*. It was like a pillow. I hugged her again and she laughed, and it felt like the jacket was warm and living. It felt like the jacket was hugging me, but since she was wearing it she must have felt like it was hugging her, too. All of our clothes hug our bodies. How wonderful to think that we are always being held by these fabrics. Our fabric family.

My sweet YouTube friend was there, too. He was so kind for bringing me. He was shining brightly because of the wonderful butterfly bike he was riding. What a *beautiful* bike. How did they get the wheels to light up? Everything was lighting up! The lights all felt so warm, and I was so glad to have those lights around me. I bet there are lights within me. I bet our cells are wrapped in lights. Someone should make a room that looks like a cell but all the mitochondria are lights.

We walked into a room filled with jellyfish. Real jellyfish[13] were floating above us! But they didn't sting? How marvelous to find these jellyfish that didn't sting! Where had they come from? I loved those jellyfish. I loved those people. My friends.

Then we walked into a room filled with mirrors. Strange, the mirrors weren't mirroring me. Or were they? My face looked different than I thought it looked. When I raised my hand, it didn't look like it was being raised in the right direction. That room was strange.

"I don't like it in here," said the Girl Who Wandered Over.

---

13 They were umbrellas with Christmas lights attached.

She was right. This room was not as inviting as the jellyfish room. Were they going to light the bonfires soon? We should go toward the bonfires. They were so bright, and there was so much smoke. And so many people. Too many people? I wanted to be alone. I couldn't stop thinking about that weird mirror. Was I myself only when I was with other people? Could I be myself alone? Did I have a self alone?

I'd be fine. I just needed to take a walk. Walking always worked. Walk until you see a new perspective. *Like an ant crawling along the surface of an orange.* That's what Mom always said. You may not see a way out, but you can always change your perspective.

My eyes hurt. I needed to look at something else.

I walked into the desert, away from the burn and away from camp. It felt colder out there, and the lights from camp were specks on the horizon. Brighter than specks. The fires looked like fireflies from there, but they were nothing compared to the sky.

Woah.

I lay down on the playa to look at the stars. It was so dark, and the stars were so bright. I was alone.

"But I'm not afraid," I whispered into the night.

I spread my arms out to make a dirt angel, feeling the earth below and the sky above me.

"Thank you."

I heard something crack beside me. I thought of Mom again.

You know what another word for fear is, Hannah? Intelligence.

Probably time to walk back.

I stood up and headed back to camp, feeling the judgment creep back in as they had said it would. I had wandered a little too deep into the dark desert night, and I wanted to be back with my friends and the lights and sounds. But I was also feeling ready for bed. A healthy distance between my desires and my actions was returning. The difference between impulse and instinct was being restored in my mind. What did I need? I think I needed to sleep. My lips were chapped, and I was thirsty.

I saw the people from my camp and the girl. They were standing in a tight circle, and no one looked very pleased.

"Hey, guys."

"Hey. Cool, so do you wanna keep rolling? We were just talking about heading over to the rave camp—"

"They used to call it Techno Ghetto."

"Whatever, so do you wanna keep rolling or—?"

I didn't have to think about it for very long.

"No, thanks. I think I got what I came here for. I still feel pretty good and I leave early in the morning, so I think I'm just gonna head back and sleep. But thank you. Thanks for everything."

I hugged the girl. But now her jacket felt itchy and stiff. It wasn't really very fluffy. The fur was matted. Reality could be so strange.

By the time I was back in my tent it was almost 4 a.m. I was leaving at 8 a.m., but I didn't think I would sleep much. I didn't write anything in my journal that night, but I lay awake for a long time trying to remember what it had been like to live without judgment. Trying to remember what it had been like to live without fear.

After that experience, which felt so complete, I decided never to do MDMA again because I didn't want to tarnish what felt like a perfect memory. These days, as hokey as it sounds, the closest I can get to regaining the feeling of peace I found in the desert is through meditation. I use an app called Headspace that offers guided meditation and makes the practice easy and approachable. I'll sit in a chair while I listen and visualize myself in that space in the desert between earth and sky, in that moment where I felt so connected to both. I try to meditate on that feeling so I can keep it with me. I want to be able to recapture it whenever I need it. That's the goal I'm working toward. Drugs are just an artificial way of getting to that feeling. They're like a shortcut. Only that shortcut can change you. And the feeling it produces is only temporary.

But achieving a sense of inner peace is real. It's out there. You just have to be willing to walk past the darkness, and even past the light, to find it.

CASUAL TRAVEL ASSHOLE

I spend a lot of time on planes. So much that I've taken to calling myself a Casual Travel Asshole. What is a Casual Travel Asshole? Well, it's someone who takes their travel plans casually but seriously. And insists on telling everyone around them about all the minor ways that they, too, could improve their travel experience! That's where the asshole part comes in. Because apparently some people feel "judged" when you observe and offer feedback without it being requested. But I just can't help myself! Knowledge is meant to be shared! For example, if I've discovered that buying a liter of water preflight and making sure to finish it by the end of any flight three hours or longer is a surefire way to stay hydrated . . . shouldn't I tell everyone I know? Or that life is so much easier when you keep all your charged electronics in one bag? And to keep that bag in your backpack (never checked) just in case your flight is delayed?

That's not all. Once I heard that flight attendants put Neosporin in their nostrils to keep from getting sick . . . let's do that, too! Nose goop for everyone!

I'm so vocal about my tested methods of travel comfort because I think everyone deserves a comfortable travel experience. Flying doesn't have to be miserable! There are measures you can take to make sure you're not sitting in a self-induced stress tank for the duration of your time in the sky.

Here are some of my tips and tricks:

1. Think of your luggage and your backpack as two separate items with two separate purposes. Luggage = things you'll need during your trip. Backpack = things you'll need during your flight. Think of your carry-on as your in-flight toolkit. What needs to be in there for the next three hours? Deodorant? Gum? A copy of *Buffering: Unshared Tales of a Life Fully Loaded?* Only carry the essentials.

2. Charge your devices before your flight. These are the stresses that we can avoid, people! A dying phone battery is one of them. It's still a good idea to pack your chargers in your backpack, though.

3. Cater to your senses! Flying is a whole-body experience. We have a tendency to think only about visual ways to entertain ourselves (books, laptops, games, and so on), but what about the other parts of your bod? Smell, sound, taste, and touch? Keeping the senses happy is equally important on your journey!

And Lord knows that an ill-timed fart from the person sitting next to you can turn minutes into hours and hours into days. But you can be prepared! Here's what I do:

SMELL: As someone with a sensitive little nose, bad smells on a plane drive me up a wall. Like the guy next to you who sleeps with his mouth wide open as you try not to think about his warm dank breath gently penetrating your airspace. Good god, how I wish that guy had drunk more water today.[1]

    CASUAL TRAVEL ASSHOLE SAYS: Carry some eucalyptus balm with you on the plane, and if something near you is invading your senses, just rub it under your nose. Peppermint oil also works great for this, but it kind of burns, so don't put it directly on the skin under your nose.

SOUND: Babies crying, humans talking, etc. If you're noise sensitive or just wanting to zen out on a plane, sounds can really aggravate. Especially when you're listening to people behind you discuss their political beliefs while you're flying to St. Louis to speak at a

---

1   There is a certain olfactory quality to dehydrated breath that I can always identify. Same as when somebody hasn't eaten enough that day. Their breath just starts to smell like their empty stomach cavity: rank and nutrient deprived. People think I'm offering them snacks and water to be kind, and that's partially true. But I'm also being kind to myself because GOOD GOD, YOUR SPIT SHOULDN'T BE SO FROTHY AND THICK. The inside of my head is a fun place. I swear.

college and you just wanna turn around and ask them some very basic questions about where all their anger and hate comes from.

CASUAL TRAVEL ASSHOLE SAYS: Use earplugs. Or if you're fancy, get some noise-canceling headphones. But those things make me feel like I have motion sickness for some reason, so I avoid them. I like earplugs since they're so cheap! And also fun and squishy. Plus, if you buy a pack and stick them in your travel bag, you'll have a backup plan when you lose your fancy headphones. Set yourself up for success, homie!

TASTE: Speaking of motion sickness, do you get queasy during takeoff and landing? Are you someone who finds airplane dining options either unsatisfying or costly or both? Same. My hunger is a precious gift. I can't waste it on those sad substitutes.[2]

CASUAL TRAVEL ASSHOLE SAYS: Oranges are great! Not only do they smell nice and taste delicious, peeling them is a nice little activity to pass the time. Plus the people around you will say "That smells so nice!" For the nausea, though, bring some minty stuff. Gum not only helps with the ear-popping during pressure changes but also soothes the tum.

---

2 I gotta say, though, Virgin America has a PB&J on flights and it's just delightful.

TOUCH: Do you feel gross and grimy when you arrive at your destination? As though your body has somehow become a wasteland of oily filth? As though your hands have never been clean before and never will be again? Also your armpits? Also your neighbor's armpits?

CASUAL TRAVEL ASSHOLE SAYS: Baby wipes, yo! Or makeup wipes! Or specifically butt wipes! Stick a pack of wipes in your backpack and give yourself a quick once-over in the bathroom before you land. It will make you feel SO MUCH BETTER. Planes always make me feel like I'm a Sasquatch, and since I've starting wiping my face (and reapplying moisturizer) during a flight—well, I just feel like it's the dawn of a brand-new day. Wipe your ears, too, for an extra-special wake-up kick!

Now, it's not that flying is always a delight when you heed these tips. I'm still not always in a happy place when I get on and off a plane. But they do help. Before I started doing these things I found myself prone to almost constant internal complaints[3] and panic attacks. Even when flying in first class! I know, I know, unbelievable, right? What right do I have to complain about luxury accommodations? Well, here's the thing: if you're the type of person who is logging internal complaints 99 percent of the time, it's not actually about the outside circumstances, it's about your internal head space. Think about it . . . what are the odds that you're *actually* constantly surrounded by idiots?

---

3 Let's not call them complaints, let's call them "moody observations."

Or that *everyone but you* is sooooo inconsiderate? Or that people really move too slowly or that seats are too small or whatever it is that's contributing to that negative monologue in your head. Guess what? If you're someone who likes to complain and be negative, ain't nothing gonna change that but you. Even if you're in first class.

Some observations on first class:

* Sometimes they have glass glasses. Isn't that nuts? And here I couldn't take my tweezers through security.

* People in first are usually less friendly, to be honest. Somehow people up front seem EXTRA aware of any encroachments into their personal space. Meanwhile, as I type this from coach, Mr. Sleepy Mouth Breather and I are basically spooning.

* The food is way way better. That's just a fact.

* Everybody is drinking.

* Sometimes they can make frothy coffee drinks!!!!!![4]

* Everybody gets blankets and pillows. No questions asked. It could be 2 p.m. on a one-hour flight from LAX to SFO, but there are your blanket and your pillow just in case you need to have a lil snuggle.

* Oh yeah, and it costs about ten times as much as coach.

That's about all you need to know. You can thank your friendly Casual Travel Asshole. What got me here? What was the turning

---

4 CAPPUCCINOS IN THE SKY!!!!

point where I decided that I just couldn't stand to be miserable on flights anymore? Especially if I was going to be flying multiple times in a month? Well, many things, but one of the contributing factors was a very scary flight I took from Reno to Colorado.

SPOILER ALERT: To this day I refuse to connect via the Denver airport.

I find flying to be terrifying in the same way that most of life can be startling—it's not the pain itself but it's the anticipation/expectation of pain that leads fear to be so exhausting for me.

I find that the closer I get to being the person I want to be and leading the life I wish to lead w/o self-loathing or guilt, I find myself a mix of peace and persistence:

If this life ends, at least it has been good.

I don't want my life to end because I think there is potential for so much good to be given. I want to spread myself around like jam on toast.

But not in a sexual sort of way. There is just so much to do. Much left to be done.

Flying is scary. It's crazy and unnatural. And as someone who was raised to believe that an apocalypse was coming to wipe out the sinners of the earth during my lifetime, flying only got scarier the more I lived out my sinful wretched life (of, ya know, not being a Jehovah's Witness). In my mind, some sort of catastrophe situation in the sky seemed like a perfect scenario for divine retribution. And I definitely deserved that.[5]

And if I was going to die for my sins, there was no time I deserved it more than during my flight back to New York via Denver after my Burning Man trip.

When I got to the Reno airport I was still riding high after my mind-expanding, judgment-free night in the desert. I boarded my flight and sat down in my seat, aware (but not anxiously self-aware) that I looked a little silly in my dusty Burner clothes. The older couple sitting next to me looked a little hippy-dippy themselves, so we exchanged some pleasant words and settled in for the flight. There was no in-flight entertainment on the plane, which was fine because I had brought a book along that I hadn't cracked at camp, and I looked forward to the simple and pleasant experience of reading on the flight. After all, I was in a state of impenetrable peace. A peace I would carry with me throughout my whole life, right?

WRONG.

---

5   No, I didn't.

I don't know if it was the weather or the temperature or what, but as soon as we left Reno and started making our way across Nevada, the airplane was bobbing like a boat tethered to the shore. Slow, constant motions that made me immediately nauseous and rendered any reading impossible. I heard people behind me who "didn't normally get sick on flights" asking the flight attendants when the rocking motions would end because they were starting to get a little sick to their stomachs. I managed to ask for a ginger ale before the captain came on and asked the flight attendants to take their seats for safety. A bone-chilling announcement every time.

With the flight attendants safely tucked away and no respite from the rocking in sight, I tried taking deep breaths to quell the churning of my stomach. I was covered in a cold sweat and the air coming out of the vent above me was none too refreshing, as it only recycled the panicked panting of the other passengers.

Then the rocking stopped, or rather it changed. It changed into bumps. Bumpy bumps. Nonstandard bumps that made people gasp aloud at the sudden drops and dips the plane was taking.

Not me, though. I wasn't gasping.

I was too busy clenching my jaws so tightly it almost made my ears ring. My warped thinking at the time was telling me that I had clearly had too much fun on the trip and had felt a little too safe and a little too happy. Plus the drugs I'd done—clearly that warranted punishment.

My mind was feverishly praying to Jehovah and apologizing for the countless sins and failures of character my life was marred with. I was wretched, and this was how I was going to die. How foolish and selfish for me to think that I could know a sense of peace on Earth when truly the only peace was in the Kingdom of Heaven. Luckily, since I was going to die *before* the apocalypse, I would have a better chance of being brought into Paradise.

"Attention passengers. We will be attempting descent into the Denver airport."

Attempting descent? What the fuck kind of announcement was that? What other conversations was this pilot having to make him think that he could update us like that and it would be enough?

I went from a state of anxiety into despair. Who would take care of my family when I was gone? What about my mom? What about Maggie? Oh, Maggie, my angel! My sun! She'd be so sad to lose me! If only I hadn't been so evil during my lifetime and wasn't now being wiped off the Earth by heavenly justice!

That was my loathing-fueled mantra as we began our descent. Or rather our attempted descent, as the air and the plane couldn't seem to agree on how they were going to work through this together. We circled the airport and tried to descend multiple times, each one equally terrifying and leading me to yet another round of internal flogging for my deviant nature. Eventually the captain came over the intercom to tell us that we had been advised to forgo attempting further entry into the airport. We had been circling in the sky for so long that we were running out of fuel and needed to undergo an emergency refueling via an airport in Nebraska.

Got it. Emergency refueling. My God.

In my head I made a plan to call Naomi from whatever airport we made it to in Nebraska to see if she could help me get on another flight, direct back to NYC. I certainly wasn't getting back onto this doomed death box. A new plane might be my only chance of salvation.

Before I could finish that thought I realized that we were landing—on dirt. *We were landing on a dirt runway.*

The refueling wasn't taking place at an actual functioning commercial airport, but at this—where were we? In a field? To this day I still don't know. I can only assume it was some sort of field for private planes. It was very confusing.

During refueling we were not allowed off the plane, but we could stand and move around the cabin. I immediately stood up and headed for the bathroom, pulling out my phone, which I hadn't used in the last four days. There was dust from the playa lodged in the cracks, and I scoffed at myself for thinking the experience had been so full. It had been artificial and man-made. Just like this plane. Not like the Kingdom of Heaven, though. I was in full-swing Jehovah's Witness mind-fuck mode.

The phone still had a charge, and I called Naomi and was angry and pissy and moody (behaviors from me that she is very used to). I told her about my original plan of finding a new flight and how my original plan couldn't work now because we weren't actually at an airport. I was furious.

"Sounds like a really scary experience, honey. I'm sorry to hear this is happening . . . I'm so glad you're safe." Naomi's soft tone sounded like pity to me and only added to my pit of rage.

"Safe FOR NOW! We have to go back up and land in Denver still! Also, I've totally missed my connection!"

"Well, if the weather is that bad, sweetheart, I'm sure other planes haven't left Denver either. You might still be able to make your flight connection. Want to send me your flight info?"

"Ugh. Fine. Yeah, I guess. Bye."[6] I hung up abruptly before send-

---

6   That is actually how rude I can be to Naomi. She is the only person on the planet I treat with such little patience. She's a saint for putting up with it, and I'm working on my anger. It's a process.

ing the text and shifting my phone into airplane mode, despite the fact that we were still on the ground. I was angry and feeling unreasonable, and I didn't want to have any further contact. First anger, then guilt, then isolation. That was the only pattern I knew.

If I had been able to talk about my feelings and understand them better at the time, I might have called Naomi and let myself cry a little. I think a more compassionate version of myself would have understood what I was really feeling and would have said something along the lines of: "I'm really scared on this flight and I don't know how to comfort myself. I don't think we were ever taught. Mom's fears were delusions, and Dad's answer to everything is 'turn to Jehovah.' But I can't pray to Jehovah anymore because I'm trying to break free of that mind-controlling doctrine and live my life. I've been so happy lately. I think I'm on the right track, but now I'm having this terrifying experience and I don't know what to do."

She would have understood that. Because a lot of that has been her journey, too.

Instead I huffed back into my seat and sat in dread, waiting for takeoff.

The hippy-dippy couple next to me was looking at the window and talking about the fields. They were old and tanned and gray, and they seemed so relaxed about sitting on this runway. I couldn't understand why. So I asked, "Excuse me, do you . . .um . . . fly a lot?"

The man turned to me smiling and said not really but since they lived in Boulder, Colorado, when they did fly it was usually into and out of Denver.

"Is it always this bad?"

"Not always. But sometimes. Just like everything else."

We took off again and encountered similar turbulence. That

time, the gentleman offered me some advice for coping with feelings of fear. He said that when he got scared he just focused on the feeling of his body in the chair and thought of his breathing and of the air going into and out of his lungs. I didn't realize it at the time, but he was teaching me how to meditate. It's a good thing that he didn't say the word "meditation" because in my mind (at the time) I wasn't buying into anything that was associated with a higher self. I would have rejected his advice flat out. Only very recently have I started to meditate daily (or at least semidaily) and the difference it has made in my life is immeasurable. I'm telling you, guys, download Headspace! Ten minutes a day! Totally achievable!

We landed safely, and I turned my phone back on to begin my series of apology texts to Naomi. I wondered how many times she would forgive me. I wondered if this was the last. My mental whip was finding its way back into my hand already. If she didn't want to talk to me, that was fine. That's what I deserved. But instead there was already a message waiting for me from her:

"Hey boo, sorry about your flights. I know how scary that can be. I checked and there are no more departures. Wanna give me a call and we'll get you set up with a hotel room?"

That night I slept at my first airport hotel. Naomi ordered me a pizza, and we googled the Denver airport to find out why flights coming into it were so bad. We researched all the conspiracy theories associated with it: everything from the layout of the runway (which some think looks like a Nazi swastika) to the art within the airport seeming "a little too alien."

The conspiracies were radical, but I was comforted to hear what others thought. Sharing knowledge, sharing resources, gotta love the Internet for that.

My friend once said he wasn't scared on planes because "turbulence is just like a car driving over a dirt road."

Since that experience I've learned about where the pockets of "rough air" are in the continental United States. I've flown back and forth so many times that knowing this helps me understand what is "normal" over certain mountain regions and certain climates. Before, I would turn every flight into a dance with death and use it to reinforce my fear-based beliefs about the world. But now I find comfort in seeking to understand the things that scare me instead of hiding from them.

My aunt once told me that she isn't scared on planes because "the pilot wants to live, too." At the time she said it I thought, "Well, why should I trust that pilot? Who knows what that guy is like?"

But now I agree with her. Flying is a mutually agreed upon act of trust between passenger and pilot. And that's kind of beautiful, when you think about it. So instead of filling the plane with your anxious energy, why not send out good vibes of calm and trust? Instead of distracting yourself or popping a Xanax, why not sink deep into the feelings and wade through them? If your heart is racing, slow your breathing. Don't ignore your body just because your mind is scared. Your mind is a tool that can bring your body peace.

These days, during scary moments on a flight (of which there are still many), I repeat in my head "safe" and "trust" and think about the pilot. I just breathe and repeat and send some good vibes their way.

If all that sounds too hippy-dippy to you, reread the beginning of this chapter and focus on those physical comforts first. Might be less complicated once you've got your earplugs and your minty gum.

KEEPSAKE

My mother always told us that there are no bad guys in this story. That things are more complicated than one person who was wrong or one person who was selfish. After Maggie was removed from our house, the courts said she could go and live with David, her father and my stepdad, as long as he didn't live with my mother.

For some reason, David didn't fight for Maggie. He decided to stay with my mother. Maybe he thought Maggie would be better off as far away from both of them as possible. Maybe he didn't want to abandon my mother because he knew she'd end up homeless if he did. Maybe he wasn't done trying to get through to her.

Sometimes it's just easier to decide that someone is the bad guy. But the truth is never that simple. Hindsight is 20/20. Everyone has a clear view from the rearview mirror.

David came into our lives when I was in third grade. He drove a vintage Mercedes just like my mom did (but hers didn't run anymore), and he spent a lot of time working on it. He was a handsome man with almond-shaped eyes and a wide smile. "He looks like Val Kilmer" was what my mother said when they first met. Everybody who met him liked him. Except for Rachel's mom. She said that handsome men don't stay handsome for long. Or maybe she just said they don't stay for long. Both turned out to be true.

David had studied journalism. He loved the Knights Templar, and he brought books into our house. He had served in the Gulf War and was in the National Guard on weekends. The first time we met him he arrived in uniform, wearing massive combat boots. He was tall and lean muscled. He had good teeth and a burn on his cheek from a stray artillery shell that had flown out of its cartridge. His family had lived in Germany for several years when he was a teenager, and he was fluent in German. He would open beer bottles with a wrench, but he hardly ever drank. He smoked like a chimney, though. In spite of the tough-guy exterior, he was never an imposing figure. He was open and friendly and taught me the importance of doing your "I love me's" in the mirror. He also introduced us to something called "basic cable," and when he was around the lights hardly ever went off.

He brought Matthew, one of his two sons, with him. I never met his older son. He also had a daughter, Rebecca, from his second marriage (Mom was his third). Rebecca would visit us occasionally. She and her mother had lived out of a car at one point, I'd heard.[1]

Rebecca's hair was platinum blond, and she had David's dark

---

1   This probably should have been a red-flag for David's type of woman.

brown eyes. She had an incredible singing voice and performed in theater. We were the same age, both seven, when we met. I felt as though I had a new sister, and the first time she came to the house I told her that what was mine was hers. That day we made a mix tape together with a tape recorder and attempted to build a teepee in the backyard. It was a wonderful first introduction and first visit, I thought, but as she hugged me when she left to go home, she said, "My daddy is going to leave you and come back to me."

I was used to adults being confusing. But never children.

After that experience I kept my distance from Rebecca, and a few years later I actually did get a new sister: Maggie.

When Mom told us that she was pregnant, I was mortified. My exact response was "We can't have a baby in this house." I was ten at the time and would be entering middle school the following year. I knew that our house was no place for a baby. Maybe not even a place for children. I had started to sneak out and had tried a joint for the first time that I'd gotten from my friend's older brother. Or rather, I think it was a joint. He called it a "strawberry doobie," and I was too scared to actually smoke it, but I did put it in my mouth unlit. So bad-ass.

Whether or not my mom should keep the baby was a debate between my mom, Naomi, and me that we discussed at length. She and David were out of their honeymoon period, and their marriage was becoming rocky. I told my mom that she should get an abortion. She'd had an abortion once, before Naomi was born. She told us that the baby would have been named Ariel.

A week or so later, Naomi awoke one morning, saying she'd just had a dream about being in a baseball stadium watching a child blow bubbles. The child was named Ariel. I assumed Naomi was lying. Naomi insisted she wasn't. But true or not, her dream tipped the scales and the decision was made. We were going to have a baby.

Once Maggie was born, our little family was renewed. The baby turned out to be a constant source of joy. She smelled like a kitten. We sang to her, smiled at her, kissed her, cuddled her, and loved her the best we could. Maggie's birth gave me a sense of purpose nothing else ever had. I stopped sneaking out after she was born. Teaching her and keeping her and protecting her from unknown hazards was a mantel I was glad to take up. But truth be told, I didn't do the best job because I was a child, too.

I started staying home from school a lot in those early years of Maggie's life to make sure someone was keeping an eye on her. Annette's neglect was worsening. If I went to school, I'd sit in class counting the seconds, and then I'd jump on the bus and scramble back home as quickly as I could.

Once I walked into the house and found Maggie (almost a year old) sitting on the floor eating a box of cigarettes. I dropped my bag and scooped her up under one arm so I could shove my finger down her throat with the other. She was squirming and fighting my hand as she gagged. Her vomit was a thick, mucuous-y blend of tobacco and milk. Then I held her and let her sob out her snotty, tear-stained feelings of betrayal. I just rocked her and said, "I know, I'm sorry. I know, I'm sorry," until her cries subsided.

I remember thinking of the incident with the aspirin in that moment. Looking around the house, it became crystal clear to me what Maggie's path would be if we stayed here. It would be like my own, which was not a life I wanted for her.

Maybe it was due to the sense of possibility that a baby can bring, but I was hopeful that we could do better with a fresh start. We'd just need a different house to do it in.

I didn't know they were going to tear it down."

I was sitting in David's car, looking at the reflection through the passenger-side mirror at a large pile of rubble where our house had once stood. Over the summer, my mom had sold our house and moved us into a new one in a better neighborhood. Our new house was closer to the high school where I would be a freshman in the fall, and it was supposed to be a move for the better. But somehow I missed our old house, and I'd asked David if we could drive by on the way home.

"I don't think there was any way they could have salvaged it," David said as he parked the car. "I'm going to go take a look."

"I'll wait here."

"Are you sure? Come on, sweetheart."

Our family was big on pet names. Everyone was sweetheart or sweetie or honey or my love or my little love, which is what I called Maggie.

"I don't want to go."

"Okay. But you might want to take a piece of it. You grew up in that house, honey. It'd be good to grab a keepsake." He got out and crossed the street to talk to the contractors.

I kept staring at the pile of rubble in the mirror. The mirror's edges created a kind of rusted vignette around the rubble. It seemed appropriate. Old. Decaying.

I started pulling the orange stuffing through the cracks in the leather seat. I wanted David to hurry up. He was talking to a group of workers standing next to the pile. He pulled out a cigarette and lit it.

That was the signal that let me know we might be there for a while. David could make conversation with everyone and anyone.

I watched their conversation in the mirror and cranked the window down. It was hot and the window stuck. David's car was cool to look at—the exterior was in primo condition—but the insides weren't up to snuff.

As I sat back in my seat to wait it out, I caught a glimpse of myself. I looked angry. Was I angry? I was. No one had told me the house was going to be demolished. No one had told me I should say good-bye. I was angry with myself for not thinking of that possibility sooner. I felt like we were abandoning a family member. The house had been a wreck, but it was our wreck. There were stains on the walls and broken glass in the door frames. I'd just figured the new owners would fix it up and fill it with happy memories.

Not tear it all down.

David gestured back toward the car, and the workers turned to look and nodded their heads. He was probably telling them I was refusing to get out. I felt as though I was being childish. But I was also feeling too much to understand. Suddenly my throat was tightening and I had to get out of the car for some air.

As I crossed the street, I tried to picture what the corner had looked like with the house still there. The plot of land and pile of broken wood and detritus looked so much bigger than the house had ever felt. So much space in the space left behind.

I waved and smiled as I walked past them and across the patches of dead dry grass. The path and the red concrete steps were still there, but now they led to nothing. I squatted to look for "a keepsake" as David had suggested. Maybe there was something here worth saving.

Some of the scraps of wood looked like paint chips. White and yellow. Our house was white when it was first built, and when we moved in—just Mom, Naomi, and me—I would sit on the front porch and pick at the paint. It came off in big chunks, taking off the wood beneath it and leaving behind strange shapes, like dragons, swords, and trees. After David and Mom got married, they decided to repaint the house. New beginnings. A fresh coat. We chose yellow because it's a happy color. It was my favorite color and still is.

What would make a good keepsake? A chunk of wood? Or would it just keep deteriorating? Maybe it would be better to just leave the whole pile to rot together. Then I remembered: the pepper tree. I got excited at the thought of the massive pepper tree that lived in our backyard. Its roots were like cradles. Always shady in the summer time. Seedpods all over the inside of our house because I would go and pull off its massive fronds and bring them in to take them apart. Baby botany.

Instinctively, I moved toward the backyard, but then it occurred to me that if the pepper tree had still been standing I'd be able to see it. Because there was no house now to block my view. The pepper tree was gone, and a thickness was building in my chest and throat. I felt as though I were suffocating. Being outside the car didn't help. Standing there wasn't helping.

"I'm going to walk to the new house. I'll see you later."

David turned. "Are you sure? Come on. I'll drive you."

He put out his cigarette under his boot. I wondered how many cigarette butts there were in that pile of pieces.

We got back into the car, and David was being kind. "You okay? I'm sorry your mother didn't tell you. There wasn't much left in the house that they could save."

I suddenly felt guilty. I'd burned and broken things in that house, and I'd punched the walls and let mold grow.

"It's not her fault. We didn't take good care of the house . . . but I really loved it."

I started to cry, and David slid across the bench seat to hug me. "You're a good person, Hannah. You're the best of any of us. You'll take care of so many things."

David always said things like that to me. I never understood why. Things were better with David in the picture. He brought us 99-cent burgers. He brought us MREs[2] from the National Guard, and I loved the tiny Tabasco bottles that sometimes came with them. I'd had a collection of them. With David there, Mom was less lonely, the house was more lively. We would sing Christmas carols anytime. David would say, "Ice cream is a food group," buy it by the gallon, and eat it with a serving spoon while we watched *The X-Files* or *Star Trek* as a family. He loved chocolate sauce and ketchup.

We started to drive away, and I asked him for a cigarette. He said he wasn't comfortable giving me one but that I could take one if I really wanted to. Suddenly I didn't want it. I appreciated the offer, though.

"You know, I love you a lot. I think I love you more than my dad. I feel like you're my real dad."

"I'm not."

"I know, but that's how I feel."

"I'm not your dad. We're friends. We're family. But I'm not your dad. Your dad is a good man. He's just not here."

"Yeah, but you're here."

David didn't reply. I realized that I hadn't taken a keepsake. Maybe there was a metal "0" from the numbers on the house buried in that pile. But David was quiet now, and I felt awkward asking him to turn back. I sighed. What was the point of keeping a fragment of something that was already gone?

---

2   Meals Ready to Eat: military rations that come in sealed brown plastic bags.

In the fall of 2004, shortly after my eighteenth birthday, Rebecca committed suicide. She was seventeen. Mom's psychosis was worsening, and the moments when no one could understand or contain her outnumbered the moments that resembled normalcy. The spaces between episodes were growing shorter, with delusion and paranoia spreading over her mind the way coffee stains a letter when spilled—the ink blurs, but you can still see traces of the words. At that point, David had left the National Guard and had started growing his hair long and trying out different forms of holistic healing. His passion for cars continued to grow, and he went to car shows a lot, as many as he could find. He also started gambling, which ate up the last of the money from selling the old house.

I think Rebecca's death was the straw that broke David's broad back. I remember my mom arriving at Berkeley and coming upstairs to my freshman dorm. I was shocked that she was there. Shocked and confused when I got the call from the door monitor downstairs, who told me there was a woman who said she was my mother there to see me.[3] I went down and took her to my room, and she told me Rebecca had shot herself in the head. I was horrified. She said we needed to go to Santa Cruz to tell Naomi in person together. I skipped my classes and drove down with her.

The reality of Rebecca's death didn't set in until we tried to eat. We stopped at a diner, and I ordered chicken soup because I had no

---

3   That would happen again in 2008, when I was living in Hoyt Hall. A freshman came to my room, knocked, and said, "There's a woman at the door who says she's your mom?" Knowing that Annette was homeless, I rushed downstairs and spent the day driving her around to shelters and service centers in the East Bay. Either she refused to enter, or they refused to take her unclean and unmedicated. I eventually drove her back across the bay and dropped her off near a shelter but told her I had to go back to school. She begged me to let her live in my car. I drove away.

real appetite. I looked down into the soup and thought, "Rebecca will never eat anything again."[4] I started to cry, and Annette said, "We don't really know she's dead. They do this to people, Hannah, they take their bodies—" I stopped crying and wrote what Annette was saying on a napkin. I left the napkin behind.

When I saw David, it was after he'd gotten back from identifying her body in the morgue. He said it looked as though she was sleeping. Her button nose with its upturned tip. He described the hole in the side of her head as a perfect circle against her temple. Coming from the military and having his fair share of exposure to guns, he described the entry and exit wounds in detail. He said he could tell that she wasn't trying to miss. As he told me this—his eyes sharp and unblinking—I thought he looked a little manic himself.

The funeral was in New Orleans. (I'm not sure why. Maybe they had family there.) Annette went with David, and, to be honest, she was being pretty monstrous to David at the time. But he stuck around for four more years, until his grief had destroyed the last of his patience for her and, with that, the last of his love. He filed for divorce, was assigned to pay spousal support, and then disappeared.

I was twenty-one and trying to finish school when we last heard from him. It was over e-mail: September 29, 2008, at 6:20 p.m. The economy was crashing and people were losing jobs left and right, and he wrote us to say that he had lost his and would no longer be able to keep paying my mom spousal support because he could barely

---

4 I think about Rebecca when I listen to Sia. I think she would have loved Sia. I think she could have sung like Sia. But now she'll never know Sia's music. I guess this is a message for those of you who contemplate permanent solutions to temporary problems. You never know what could be coming in the future. There is so much music you've yet to hear.

meet his own rent/utility/food/gas obligations. He said that he would be completely unemployed by Friday. He apologized and described how he was trying to find work.

The e-mail was sent to my mother, but Naomi and I were CC'ed. He wrote to us directly at the end of it saying that he had done his best and he was including us on this message so we would know our mother was in trouble. He was still trying to help.

I never replied to that e-mail. My mother, on the other hand, wrote thousands of e-mails to David from the library. They were all roughly the same; here is one of them:

From: Annette

Date: Wed, Jan 23, 2008 at 5:59 PM
SUBJECT: love
To: David
CC: Hannah Hart

"Marry me and

share my name." David C. Whitney Jr. Spring of nineteen ninety

four. We met in October of nineteen ninety

three.

In October of this year we will have known each other for fifteen years of our children's lives. Hannah and

Rebecca were seven years old. Maggie is now ten. "We'll grow old together and laugh while we watch each

other fall apart." I love you.

David disappeared after that. He changed his phone number. Something I understand. Annette's tendency was to call non-stop until your voice mail was full. Then, as soon as you cleared it out, she'd begin again. She does that with me, too.

For his sake, I'm glad he disappeared. I don't blame him. I know it was an act of self-preservation.

So, dear reader, if you'll indulge me, I'd like to take a moment to reply to his e-mail. Just in case somehow, someday he might read this, too.

From: Hannah Hart

Date: Wed, Apr 20, 2016 at 2:45 PM
Subject: Re: Out of money
To: David

Dear David,

Thank you for trying. Thank you for trying harder than anyone else tried. I remember the holes in your shoes. I remember the hours you worked. I remember the attempts you made to get Mom into a hospital and get her help and proper care. The system is broken and I know you did all you could. I know that because I'm doing all that I can now.

Thank you for telling me I had great hair. Thank you for your songs and your tears and your encouragement and your laughter.

Maggie, Naomi, and I are doing very well. Maggie loves theatre and musicals. It hasn't been easy, but she's made it past 17 and she's an amazing young woman. She has much to be proud of. But that's her story to tell.

I think about Rebecca every day. Fresh tears. I wish I had that picture of us from the car show. I feel responsible and guilty and sad about what happened. I still feel like there was more I could have done.

They say it's called "survivor's guilt." I'm trying to turn that guilt into gratitude. Her death taught me such value for life. I hope it taught you the same.

With love and understanding,

Hannah

SHADOWBOXER

Sometimes I hear my father's voice saying that the Devil wants us to misplace the anger we have at this System of Things and point it towards Jehovah. It makes me feel wicked and wretched to be angry. But our Creator has not wronged me. The weakness is in myself.

—Spring 2007

As an LGBTQIA+ figure I feel a great responsibility to be as informed a representative as possible. The thoughts and views expressed in this chapter are simply a retelling of my experience of coming to terms with my sexuality. This is not doctrine on gender, identity, fluidity, or any of those realities that we are creating room for in society today. If I say anything here that offends you, please know that I'm still learning, too.

I was raised to believe gay people are sinners. All queer people, really. Growing up, I was taught that some people are gay, in the same way that some people molest children or practice bestiality. That's actually a direct quote from my father, from once when we were in Home Depot. We were doing something fun,[1] and I was young, I must have been under the age of ten. I have no idea how the issue even came up, but when he wanted to make a firm point, he didn't spend much time dancing around it.

"All sins are equal in the eyes of Jehovah," he replied.

And sinning against Jehovah really meant sinning against my father. Which was the last thing I wanted to do. All I had to do was be good enough and Christian enough, and maybe one day he would say "You know what, girls? Life is looking a little rough for you, and

---

1   There was always something to be done for the house: gardening, home repair, building, or organizing. I loved it because it meant going to Home Depot and maybe we could get one of those incredible hot dogs. Hope hope hope!

I'm worried about your mother. Let's combine our powers and try to tackle this stuff as a family."

Instead when he picked us up for a visit he told us that we needed a bath.

It's hard for me to revisit all the fear and judgment I held in my heart. All the loss I felt in coming to terms with my sexuality. The loss of my faith, the loss of my father, the loss of so many things just to have this one small, insignificant thing.[2]

Or at least that's how I thought about it at the time.

I first learned what "being gay" meant after my Grandpa Peter, Dad's father, had an accident and ended up in the hospital. Naomi and I were spending the weekend with Dad, and we were planning to go clean out Grandpa's apartment while he was recovering. Before we left my father took us into the backyard to talk to us about something very serious. Serious and dark and shameful. He sat on the picnic table while I stood on the bench. He was probably only a little older than I am now. He looked somber and sad. A single father with his daughters for the weekend and an aging father he had to take care of. I'm sure he was overwhelmed.

He told us that Grandpa Peter was an alcoholic (and later he said he was a speed addict?) and that he was very ill. He said that while we were cleaning out his apartment we might see some things, disgusting things, because of how sick my grandpa was. I was pretty confused, but Naomi seemed to have a better understanding of what he

---

2 Ya know. Falling in love and finding a partner and living an honest and whole life. No big deal.

meant. He then told me that Grandpa Peter was sexually attracted to little boys and if we stumbled across anything dangerous and scary we should clean a different part of the apartment or tell him so he could come and clean that area himself.

As we drove to Oakland for our big cleaning adventure, I started to imagine a lot of terrible things. My dad didn't believe in TV (so ahead of the curve!), and he really didn't have any idea of the sort of things kids could see in the media. My mother had a job transcribing the news, and since we were her only companions before David came into the picture she would tell us about all the awful things that happened in the world each day. I was convinced that children were kidnapped nightly.

We'd never been to Grandpa's apartment before. And honestly, we never saw him very much at all. So I had no idea what to expect. As we drove along, I started to imagine a locked room filled with children that my grandpa was abusing. Chains and all sorts of dark shit. Were we on a rescue mission? I guess I would have to wait and find out when we got there. I looked down at my hands and made fists and tried to imagine myself as big and not small and helpless. Maybe I could help those trapped boys. I promised myself that I would hug them no matter how dirty they were. I was dirty sometimes, too!

When we arrived, the scene was not that of a psychotic kidnapping. It was the home of an old man who was very much alone. His hobby was mycology, and he had a collection of dehydrated mushrooms. Cigarettes and bottles and hoards of objects and newspapers and magazines, all covered in a layer of grime, filled the apartment. The place *was* filthy, but Naomi and I exchanged a look when we entered that said "This looks like home."[3]

---

3   Dad's House was Dad's House. Mom's House was Home.

We cleaned without much conversation. It was gross, but frankly it was nothing that Naomi and I weren't used to. Having to clean a house from "inhabitable" to "habitable" was a biyearly event for us. My dad was tackling the kitchen. There was a lot to sort through, a lifetime of knickknacks and sundries. There was a particularly cool mushroom in a glass case that I wanted to show Naomi, so I went to find her. She was cleaning in Grandpa's bedroom.

I walked in, and Naomi was crouched over something on the ground.

"Hey, Nomes, how do they get the mushroom in there? Look."

I startled her when I approached and she grabbed my arm and conspiratorially whispered, "No. *Look.*"

What she showed me was definitely not a mushroom.

Naomi was sitting in a pile of magazines she had found. She had her hands on one with a naked man in it. She flipped it open to show me, and there were *lots* of naked men in it. They were muscled and tan and hairless[4] and just . . . naked. Naomi suggested trying to find a way to keep one, and I just couldn't stop staring, because I had never seen anything like those magazines. Was this what my dad was talking about? I was certainly shocked, but I wasn't horrified. My reaction was absent of terror. These were men, not children. Just naked pictures. What was the harm in that?

As we turned the pages, things got more complicated, with bodily fluids involved. I started to feel grossed out by the functions of the male sex and instead focused on their arms and chest and muscles. They looked so big and cool and strong. Look, this one is a

---

4 It wasn't until middle school that I learned about pubic hair. The only frame of reference I had was my own body. When I first learned that "pubes" were a thing, I was revolted. Little did I know that that would be the beginning of my lifetime battle with sensitive fair skin and thick body hair. Oy.

fireman. This one is chopping down a tree. They are doing so many things because they can. They can because they are strong. I want to go to the woods and chop. I want to be big and strong.

"Woah, this one has a girl in it."

Naomi turned the magazine to share. There was a woman with her legs spread and breasts spilling out over her shirt. Despite my limited understanding, the image was inescapably sexual. My face was hot. But it wasn't the position she was in or the flesh of her body that had transfixed me. It was the look on her face. Open mouthed and wide eyed.

Our father called for us, and we hid the magazines under the bed. I felt dirty and shameful. Naomi said we should keep it a secret. I kept a lot of other people's secrets at that time without really knowing it.

But I suppose that was the first one that was mine.

If you ask me about "the first time I thought I might be gay," I could say it was that moment. But that would be a lie, because I didn't really understand the feelings I was having when I saw that picture. There was no cognition behind the way I was reacting. It was just natural.

I might also say it was earlier, when I was in kindergarten, and spending time with the girls in my class would make me feel shiny and sparkly and I always wanted to be the prince in every story. Not out of a desire to be manly[5] but out of a desire to have a princess to save.

Or I could say it was any time I was near another girl at all and

---

5   Whatever that means.

she smelled so clean and nice and I wanted to be her favorite thing in the world.

Or I could say it was when I was in middle school and I heard that my friends' sister might be bi and I felt repulsed.[6]

Or I could say it was when I watched Britney Spears[7] do anything and felt everything.[8]

Or I could say it was the first time a boy kissed me and it was fine. ¯_(ツ)_/¯

Or I could say that it was during my senior year in high school when Ashley Arabian told me to put out my cigarette before going into a party because "boys don't like girls who smoke" and I immediately crushed it in my palm because I wanted her to like me and think I was so *so* cool.

Or it was when I realized I was having that thought and hated myself for caring so much about what Ashley thought of me and so little about the boys.

The truth is that I think it was all of those moments combined. It was in every moment. It was in every breath of my big gay lungs and every beat of my big gay heart.

Denial is both active and passive, and I fought against my truth at every move. Shadowboxing myself in my subconscious. Ducking and swinging and watching my footing to make sure I was always outpacing my true desires.

---

6 Homophobia is a big, strong indicator of gayness: *"How dare they be gay! And kiss each other . . . with those soft full lips . . . and maybe then they hold each other . . . and maybe even go to a farmer's market after exchanging mutually gratifying acts of oral sex . . . How terrible to imagine!!"*

7 My best friend's mom was the first one to call out my gayness. It was after I described an MTV performance in such detail that she asked, "Do you wanna *be* her or do you wanna *do* her?"

8 . . . in my pants.

BUFFERING

Until denial and I circled each other in our final rounds. Until I went to college and met my match.

The smell in the air is the same,
But the feeling has changed

You and I
are different now
We speak
We smile
We spend

the same time,
in the same spaces

but the air is different here,
and words travel the distance
in different ways.

And visions filter into different eyes.

But when I look at you
In the light of last summer

I can't help but remember,
How nice it felt
to have

Your hand against my face.

—Spring, 2007

Berkeley's campus is green year round, with a variety of flowers that all seem to bloom at once. That's how it looks in my memory, every moment on the verge of blossoming, every breeze laced with opportunity.

When I found out I was going to college, it was a dream come true. Not only was UC Berkeley my "reach" school, but it was the only school I applied to that had accepted me. So it must have been fate. The application process wasn't smooth, and before accepting me they asked for two additional letters of recommendation and gave me thirteen essay questions that I had to complete and return within a ten-day window. I remember walking into my yearbook class after school and talking through the application process with Mr. Morgan, one of my favorite teachers, a man whose approach and dedication to education and his students had saved many lives, including mine. (Just wanted to take a moment to appreciate this teacher. All teachers really. Big shout-out!)

Anyway, being admitted to Berkeley was great not only because of its academic reputation but also because it was in the Bay Area. I wouldn't have to leave my mother or Maggie behind; they would be only a BART ride away. I was also provided with financial aid and assistance in the form of work-study. Life was looking up.

Everything was falling into place, and I was determined not to screw it up and to do better than I ever had academically. I had been blessed, and I would not squander the gifts the Lord had provided. So freshman year I was a good Christian girl who wore a cross and lived in Freeborn Hall, the substance-free dorm on campus. That year I didn't party,[9] and I went around to Christian church groups trying to find one that was liberal enough for my political views and

---

9   Much.

had a man that I could marry. Despite dabbling in dating in high school, I had yet to fall in love or experience that head-over-heels feeling. I was determined to find a partner so my real life could begin.

At that time I also chose a major, Communications— Advertising.[10]

At that time, I also continued my studies of French.[11]

At that time, I also . . . was bullshitting myself a lot.[12]

I read more *Lord of the Rings* and Harry Potter fanfic than was healthy and kept my mind as tightly locked in a fantasy as I could. Sure, maybe I was avoiding something. But what about Draco and Harry, huh? What were they avoiding? Their love for each other??? I shipped that shiz.

When the holidays arrived, I would stay on campus and continued to work. My financial aid provided me with meal points, but when classes were out of session the dining halls were all closed. I remember one rainy week (must have been just before spring break) walking across the campus carrying boxes of instant mac and cheese I planned to make in the microwave. I'd live on that all week. Pasta never let you down. And if I wanted a real hot meal I could take the train for an hour and a half south to visit my father or back across the peninsula to visit Maggie and her adoptive family. The holidays were lonely, but when school was back in session I was happy as a clam. I loved being in the dorms because I loved being surrounded by people studying different things.

---

10 Which eventually switched to English Lit.
11 Which eventually switched to Japanese.
12 Which . . . actually, no, that stuck around for a bit longer.

During that first year at school I met one of my (to this day) closest friends, Becca. She was someone I bonded with because—well, actually, I don't know why we were so instantly fond of each other. On paper we're totally different. Becca has a very wry, dry outlook on the world, bordering on pessimistic, yet she is supportive and delightful. And hilarious.

Once I invited her to go check out some church event with me and her deadpan reply was "Jesus? On a weekday?"

Needless to say, I never did find a church that was quite the right fit. Jehovah's Witnesses were against all other forms of religion, no matter how Christian they seemed. I knew I didn't want to be a Witness (because that shit was crazy), but I still loved Jesus and God and wanted to continue my worship. I just couldn't figure out how.

As freshman year was coming to a close, and despite efforts to convince myself that I had crushes on the guys around me, I could never maintain my interest or find a spark. Still no boyfriend/future husband. I figured it was because my childhood had screwed me up. I was damaged goods. Incapable of loving anyone romantically. Possibly ever. Becoming a nun was starting to seem like an option.

But instead of moving to a nunnery I did the next best thing and moved into a sixty-person, all-female co-op. A co-op is an off-campus public house open to anyone attending a school nearby. Hoyt Hall had sixty other girls living in it and was sure to keep me chaste and safe from the Devil's fornications. I moved to avoid the boys so I could avoid being *so* tempted. Yep, nothing but me and the ladies. Safe from all physical desires. Yep. Yep. Yep.

. . .

Oh, the lies we tell ourselves.

That first fall at Hoyt Hall was very full and fast. Our co-op operated on communal labor. Everyone had "work shifts," and there were management positions along with those shifts. We each pulled our weight to maintain our home together. I shared a double room with a girl named Lana who was so brilliant and strong that we would do push-up contests as study breaks. She later learned how to fly helicopters and became a National Forest firefighter. Now she's married with babies I think. I hope she is happy and well.

Lana showed me how strong a woman could be. And I met so many other wonderfully strong and interesting people in that house: transfer students, five-year graduates, women from differing racial and socioeconomic backgrounds, women who liked to have open and frank discussions about mental health, women who knew how to cook, women who knew how to eat, women with different abilities and talents, women who struggled and triumphed. They all challenged and inspired me in every possible way.

Oh, I also met lesbians there. Bona fide out-and-proud lesbians.

Obviously, I avoided them like the plague.

But flirted with all the straight girls.

But not like . . . in a gay way, of course. Because being gay was gross. Ew.

I was just flirting with girls whom I had tingly feelings for because . . . well, you know . . . friendship?

Part of me believed I was exploring the freedom of being flirtatious on girls to prep for the boys, because anytime my flirtations with a straight-identifying girl led to a quiet confession of feelings on her behalf I would reject her and tell her that she had been misinterpreting my intentions all along.

Then, at night before bed, I would read my Bible[13] and pray. Pray for a husband, as I did every night. Pray for Jehovah to bring me a husband.

Late in the semester, before winter break crept up, I found out that I would be getting a single room in the spring. Someone joked that it would be the year when I would "for sure get some lovin'," and I'm sure I gave a thumbs-up in return. The single room was available because it was the smallest in the house (the width of a large walk-in closet), but it was the first time in my life I would have a room all to myself, so I was thrilled. A bedroom of my own design. How blessed these new beginnings were sure to be. The first night I spent in that room, I read a scripture that struck me:

> *"When you ask, you do not receive, because you ask with wrong motives, that you may spend what you get on your pleasures."*
>
> *James 4:3*

I remembered a talk in the Kingdom Hall my father had given about how we could not pray for specific things, because it might not be in God's plan for us to have them. Instead, we must pray for the strength behind those things, for the meaning behind them. I had spent more than a year and a half praying for God to help me find a husband. But maybe I hadn't found him because I hadn't been capable of it.

That night, instead of my usual prayers for a man to sweep me

---

13 King James and NIV; I'd read and compare. Made it through both.

off my feet, I prayed: "God, please help me to understand my heart. Please guide me toward love."

Someone tapped my shoulder.
"I like your jacket."
She smelled like gardenias.

During my sophomore year I dropped my French classes because I didn't want to go to France. I realized that if there was any country in the world I wanted to visit, it was Japan. The home of Sailor Moon! So I started taking Japanese classes five days a week so I could apply to study abroad in Japan the following fall.

On the first day of the new semester I sat down in Japanese class and felt a tap on my shoulder. I turned around, and the girl behind me complimented my jacket. It was a maroon jacket, made from some sort of sport material, and I felt it was too small for me—too tight across my shoulders and too narrow at my waist. I was used to wearing things that were baggy. When I turned to look at her, it felt even tighter.

"Really? Thanks! I got it from the free pile."

"What's a free pile?"

"Oh it's like this pile of free stuff in the co-op where I live. We are really big on recycling, and when you have something that's still good but that you don't need, you just put it in the free pile for someone else."

"Wow! So it's like just lots of free clothes?"

"Mostly clothes, yeah, but also other stuff. School supplies, stuff for your room—"

"Like lightbulbs?"

"Ha! Actually no, not those. We have those in the maintenance closet, so if somebody needs one for a personal lamp, I usually just let them have it. Oh, I'm the maintenance manager, by the way, so I have the key."

"Maintenance manager?" She looked confused; her face was so expressive, and also so pretty. Her features were strong but strongly feminine. It was a little distracting when she spoke because just looking at her was overwhelming my senses.

"Yeah, it's a position in the co-op . . . like a job? And then my rent is cheaper because it's a big responsibility that you fill daily, not weekly like the other work shifts. Best part is that it takes a third off the price of my rent. It's a cool system, a little complicated, but simple when you get the hang of it."

I felt like I was babbling in another language, neither English nor Japanese. But she actually seemed interested and curious. It was nice.

"I've never even heard of the co-ops, to be honest." She was polite. "But that's probably because I'm a freshman. I still live in the dorms. I was thinking about becoming an RA next year though."

"You should definitely move to the co-ops! It's great! You'd love it!"

"Would I?"

"For sure."

"And how do you know what I'd love?"

I paused.

"Well, you love this jacket, right?"

She laughed. I felt her eyes lingering on mine. She replied in Japanese, 「なるほど…」 [14]

It was incredibly sexy when she spoke like that. Wait, *sexy?*

I felt as though the wind had been knocked out of my stomach. My shadowboxer had landed a punch.

Class started, and by the end we were officially study buddies for the new semester. Her name was Emiko, and she had grown up speaking Japanese at home (her father was Japanese, and her mother was mixed). She was already fluent in the language so the classes were an easy A for her. She was just trying to brush up her skills to work toward a dual major in Japanese and Peace and Conflict Studies. I didn't even know that was a major. What a splendid major. What a splendid person.

We were still talking when we left class, and there was so much more to talk about. We had Japanese class together in the morning five days a week and lunch together more often than not. She was so driven, it was inspiring. At the time, I was working toward only one major (English Lit.) with a minor, but by the end of that first week she was convinced that I should be going for two degrees at once, just like she was. She had such faith in me.

By the end of the second week of the semester our strengths and weaknesses were aligning. Her courses were heavy in essay writing, and she was struggling because her professors told her that her essay topics "weren't complicated enough." I told her I loved to complicate things and writing always came pretty naturally to me.

---

14 なるほど: *naruhodo* : When you suddenly, or deeply, understand something or some mechanism of what someone is saying.

"I write most of my essays at five a.m. I just set an early alarm."

She scoffed, "I write most of my essays *till* five a.m., and then I sleep for two hours."

"I've never been a big fan of sleep anyway."

"I love it. I just don't get enough of it."

"Well, I can help you with your outlines and then maybe you can sleep more? You help me enough in Japanese."

By the end of the third week we both began to talk about our families and we realized we'd had similar roles at home. Children taking care of parents and younger siblings. I'd never felt such kinship with someone.

At the beginning of the fourth week I invited her to a house party my co-op was throwing. She accepted and said she was looking forward to it. Before I knew what was happening, I told her she could sleep over after the party if she wanted. She said that sounded good, too.

Oopth.

As I counted down the days to the party, my heart was racing even in my sleep. I was nervous. More nervous than I had ever been. In the face of chaos I was always focused and steadfast, but now with everything going according to plan, I was feverishly afraid.

According to plan? And what was my plan, exactly?

I couldn't sleep and I couldn't eat, and eventually my friends in the co-op took notice. Dinner was a communal event. People cooked in the house as part of their work shift, and the best cook was a woman named Anjelica.[15] She was the boss of our house. Her hair slicked back into a tight braid, she and Meredith (a proud Italian and her best friend/part-time lover) would cook *cumbia* music rang

---

15 Only her friends could call her *Jeliz*.

through the house. They had lived in the house longer than almost anyone else and were both transfer students who had met years previously. At first I avoided them because I was scared of being seen with lesbians, but as my worldview expanded, so did my friendships. We had a playful friendship, they were older and wiser and bolder, and I was precocious and curious and inept.

On the Friday of the party I skipped dinner altogether. Instead I hid out in my room, trying on different outfits. There was no mirror in my room, so I had to march to the bathroom every time I wanted to check on how I looked, staring at the floor to avoid eye contact with anyone I encountered along the way.

"Corazón! Watch it!"

Anjelica shouted from somewhere behind me. I looked up and narrowly avoided smacking into someone who was carrying a pile of decorations for the party.

I muttered "Sorry" and ran into the bathroom to check my outfit. Dissatisfied, I exited, only to see that Anjelica was still standing there.

"Come to my room and talk."

M eredith was there, too, and the conversation the three of us had changed my life. I told them everything: that I had been questioning my sexuality, that maybe I had *always* been questioning my sexuality, that there was this girl I really liked, that she was my friend and I could not stop thinking about her, and that I didn't know what to do about it because no matter what I didn't want to be gay. I was shaking as I told them and sometimes my eyes would tear up, but mostly I just couldn't breathe. Then I was being hugged—*tranquila, tranquila*—and then I was crying, but only a little because of the tightness of my jaw.

Anjelica and Meredith were patient and didn't judge me, even though I was acting as though being gay were some sort of sinful curse. After living in an all-female house for so many years, they'd seen people come to accept themselves in all sorts of ways. I apologized for avoiding them when we'd first met. It was just that Anjelica was such a bold personality and so proud about being a lesbian that I didn't think we could be friends. She laughed and told me that she'd had her struggles, too. Her family was devout Catholic and she was first generation—her parents had come to the United States from Mexico. Maybe they knew she was a lesbian, but they never talked about it.[16]

Still, I insisted that I wasn't really a lesbian and that this girl was just a big complicated mystery I couldn't solve. They didn't push me any further, which was good. I think their patience gave me enough space to eventually accept my true feelings.

By the end of our conversation, it was decided that I would talk to Emiko before the party. I wrote down what I was going to say and rehearsed it, repeating my speech as I walked to her dorm to pick her up and walk back with her to the party.

As we walked back, she kept asking me if something was wrong. I suggested stopping at a café at the halfway point between us. I did so intentionally because I figured that if things didn't go well she wouldn't have to go too far to get back to her dorm and I would already be halfway to the comfort of my friends.

We sat side by side on a curb outside the café, in the glow of a streetlamp behind us. The air was rich with night-blooming jasmine, but all I could smell was the gardenia perfume she wore.

---

16 Before she graduated, she finally told them. They came to graduation and celebrated with her and her girlfriend, now fiancée. All very warm and fuzzy.

"Is everything okay? You're making me nervous."

"Ha! No. *You* make *me* nervous!" I was a little too loud and a little too abrupt, and thank God I could improvise because that wasn't the first line of my speech. "No. Um . . . sorry, that's not what I mean. You actually make me . . . happy. Really happy. But it's the kind of happy that . . . also makes me nervous."

"I don't understand," she said gently.

"When we spend time together, it makes me feel so good. I'm so happy to have you as a friend. I'm so happy to be with you . . . but . . . I think it's because I want to be *with* you. I think. Maybe. I don't know. Sorry, this is all just kind of—"

"Ah. I think I understand."

"You do?"

"Yeah . . . I do." She reached out to touch my hand. "I get it. I feel that way, too."

"Happy?"

"Yes, happy. But nervous, too. Confused. Mostly confused."

"Right? Okay, cool. Same! Oh, my god. What's happening?" She laughed and I laughed, and it suddenly felt like the air wasn't so thin. "Do you still want to come to the party? Because it's totally okay if you don't. I actually chose to tell you here because that way this café is in between us, so if you wanted you could just walk home or I could walk you home or whatev—"

"You're just so sweet." The words fell out of her mouth as though she were exhaling, and I couldn't tell if she was talking to me or to herself.

"I try!"

We were quiet for a minute. Smiling at each other and then looking away and then looking back and smiling. Finally she said that she'd still like to go to the party, if that was all right with me. I told her of course.

The party was a blur of music and tequila and dancing, but when we stumbled into my room at the end of the night we were suddenly sober. We stayed up talking before brushing our teeth and then getting into my twin-size bed. I lay on my back while she lay on her side facing me. I was sure my heart was finally going to burst through my chest. I let out a deep breath and turned toward her.

"So, I'm just going to kiss you now, okay?"

"Yeah. That's okay."

"Great." She moved onto her back, and I leaned over her and kissed her.

She tastes like Aquafresh.

First kisses are supposed to be awkward, but I'd like to thank the heavens and whatever powers that be that this one wasn't. Somehow our mouths met perfectly and our breathing matched in time. I felt my heart and my thoughts slowing down. In fact, everything was slowing down. Everything that existed within me was settled and calm. No shadowboxers moving in tight circles. Just the feeling of her mouth and body against mine.

When I came up for a breath, somehow it was morning and somehow clothing had been removed. In the span of a few hours we had gone farther than any sexual experience I'd had. I checked the time and laughed.

"How is it eleven a.m.?"

"I have no idea."

I lay back and felt there was something I needed to ask her. "Did you . . . were you thinking about me being a girl? And you being a girl? At all? Any of that stuff?"

"Not really, no. I was . . . pretty distracted."

"Yeah, me, too."

"But I don't think I'm gay, if that's what you're asking."

"Same, yeah. Yeah, me neither. I just . . . like you."

"I like you, too."

We slept some and then had lunch before I walked her back home. Neither of us wanted to kiss good-bye in public. But it was more than enough to smile at her as she walked away. I was glad we were on the same page.

But I think that was the last time that we ever were.

She smiles after she kisses me. She's straddling my lap. I'm sitting in a swivel chair. We are surrounded by computers but I locked the door so no one could use them. She wants to say something.

"When I kiss you, your lips feel so big, but when you smile your lips disappear."

"Well, when you kiss me my heart feels so big, and when you smile everything disappears."

She rolls her eyes and calls me a poet. She smiles and kisses me again.

I wasn't gay the spring and summer that we dated. I wasn't gay when I would go down on her for hours or frankly anytime we had sex. I wasn't gay when I was watching her sleep or holding her hand in mine and thinking about what it would look like if there were rings on those fingers. I certainly wasn't gay when Pride parade came around and I would rather be caught dead than wear a rainbow or celebrate. I wasn't gay when she was telling her family about me and I was lying to mine. I wasn't gay when people asked me who I was dating because she and I weren't *dating*: we were *in love*.

Good thing was that she wasn't gay either. She was just experimenting and that's what she told everyone. Which is why she was comfortable talking about it.

But I couldn't talk about it with my family because I knew we weren't an experiment. We'd get married (as two straight women) and then and only then would I tell my family. I didn't need to say the word "gay" because this wasn't long term. I wasn't gay at all, I was simply *hers*.

It was great though, being hers. We spent so much time in my bed and in my bedroom that Lana once wrote me a note and slipped it under the door questioning if I was gay, or if I just really wanted to have sex before marriage. The implication being that sex before marriage *with a woman* simply didn't count as sex because hey, what's sex without a penis?[17]

Anyway back to being young and obsessed. I couldn't get enough of Emiko. I was just a clingy and smitten lil' homo who was by her side as often as I could be. Walking across campus in the middle of the night to hold her while she took a nap from 2–5 a.m. It was more than enough for me though. I was content to be her security blanket because my only need was needing her.

I shared with her my Faith and my nightly Bible readings. She even started attending Christian church groups of her own. She

---

17 It's hard for me to explain how much I love having sex with a woman without being labeled as man-hating. Which I find to be rather funny because I know plenty of men that don't want a dick inside them so are they man-hating too?

started attending more sermons than I did. Partly because as we fell deeper and deeper in love I was having a harder and harder time reconciling my two devotions.

A relationship can be a great mirror for your virtues . . . but also your vices. And one of mine was my total abject denial about what a shitty relationship we were actually in.

Our relationship was one large red flag. But I couldn't see it because I was being my own red flag, too. I was trying to match her step for step, but we were walking on different paths. And it wasn't until six months after being together, when I was packing to leave for Japan, that everything should have been so obvious to me, but I chose to ignore it.

"I can't believe this is over. I can't stop crying." She is crying on the couch of my sister's apartment. She gave it to us for the night so we could have some "goodbye time" before I would leave for the airport. I was angry because she kept crying about me leaving and I didn't understand why.

"Jesus. Listen, I'm only going to be gone for four months okay? That's nothing. That's it!"

"Yeah but you agreed with me when I said we couldn't keep dating."

"Well, I mean, yeah, but whatever. Just because we aren't 'together' doesn't mean we are just going to stop loving each other? Dating is just a word! Love is a state.[18] Our feelings aren't changing, the way I feel about you is going to stay the same."

---

18 Love is a verb.

She looked at me with wide wet eyes and put her face in her hands again. "Nothing is going to be the same. It's not going to be the same. We aren't going to be like this."

I was uncomfortable and so confused. She was crying so much and in my mind her pain was proof of her love for me. I started kissing her to distract myself (or maybe both of us) from what she was saying. We had sex on the couch one last time. It was very fast and fumbly and unfulfilling. Nothing like the long gazes and slow soft touching we had been doing since we met. It felt like we were already changing, and I hadn't even left yet.

Naomi drove me to the airport and Emiko couldn't bring herself to go. I texted "I love you I love you I love you" and just before I boarded my flight she wrote "I love you too" but somewhere deep down, I knew it wasn't in the same way.

The path to accepting your sexuality has to start somewhere. For those who identify as heterosexual, the childhood bliss of an early crush is typically encouraged and praised. Milestones such as your first date and the prom are celebrated by parents and friends.

But when you're anything other than straight, it's more complicated; your growth gets shrouded and stunted. That's why a lot of queer people, when they fall in love and get into a relationship for the first time, revert to a kind of prepubescent puppy love: spontaneous, impulsive, obsessive, and ecstatic. I've heard many people express annoyance at friends who "just came out and it's totally cool and whatever, but do they have to talk about it all the time?" My answer to that is "Yes. Yes, they do. Don't you remember puppy love? Well, imagine if you had to hide it for twenty years. So yeah, if they wanna gush about it, let them gush. There's a first time for everything."

For me the path to self-acceptance meant accepting heartbreak. Emiko and I dated for only six months or so, but it took me years to get over her. I devoted hundreds of journal pages obsessing over every detail of every interaction we had postbreakup. What I've learned from rereading those pages and the countless retellings of our story is that our relationship had become a kind of microcosm for my struggle to accept my sexuality as a whole. Looking back, accepting heartbreak really meant accepting who I was.

Before Emiko, I'd convinced myself that I was fractured and could never love. Figuring out that I'd actually just been raised super homophobic and thus really tortured about being a gay person. That was it. What a relief!

I'm still working on letting go of many of the dark pieces of my past, but I'm proud (out and proud!) to say that being a lesbian isn't one of them.

If you're reading this and you think that maybe you could love someone of the same gender (or nongender), all I have to say to you is this: Congratulations! You're perfect and wonderful and more alive than you ever knew. Be proud of who you are because you're already more than enough.

BODY LANGUAGE

Now that we've explored some tales of the human heart, I'd like to take a broader look and talk about the body itself. Blessedly, I've always felt aligned with my gender identity, but it took me years to understand my relationship between the presentation of that identity and presentation of myself: specifically my personal grooming and style. For me, I like to pay attention to this sort of thing because I am a lover of language and the words exchanged before any word is spoken at all.

WILDCAT

I identified strongly with my grade school mascot, the Washington Wildcat. Powerful and untamed, yet collected and docile when necessary, wildcats were aware yet unconcerned with what the other animals in the jungle were thinking. That was who I wanted to be. Unfortunately, in elementary school, I think I was more Grumpy Cat than a Wildcat—basically summed up in this photo (I'm the one in the purple shirt):

Or maybe more accurately in this photo:

Yeah, that's me.[1] Now look at the girl next to me, all shiny and bright in her flowered skirt.[2] That was not me.[3] Growing up, I was a

---

1   IDGAF = I didn't give a fuck.
2   SGAF = She gave a fuck. Or her mom did.
3   That's Jessica Couto, a sweet and awesome girl whose family was also

---

tomboy. My mom didn't force us to conform to anyone's preset no-
tions of how girls should dress, and that was kind of a blessing. The
exception was the four days a month we spent with Dad, when he
and Jenny would force us to wear itchy dresses with suffocating
tights and shoes that pinched. At home with Mom, the options were
limited and we had no rules, which usually led to my wearing the
same thing for a week at a time.

In second or third grade, a kid I'll call Andy pointed out to the
whole class that I had only one pair of jeans. He could tell because
he had been there when I fell on the playground and the asphalt had
ripped them at the knee. It was clear that they hadn't been washed
and the hole hadn't been sewn up. What he said in front of the class
was something like "Ew! Why do you keep wearing the same pants?"
I was silent and mortified.

Looking back at this photo and my dirty jeans, I'm kind of
shocked that the school never said anything. I can only imagine we
must have smelled pretty ripe at times since we didn't have a lot of
underwear in our house. We didn't own brushes either, and I can remember sitting in class and using pencils to explore the mats in my
hair. Eventually my mom would just cut them out. I've always had
thick hair, so it was never really a problem. There were always plenty
of layers to hide the missing chunks.

And I remember those shoes. God, I loved them. When we
would go to Goodwill or look through the donation bags that filled our
house, I always kept my eyes peeled for shoes with Velcro. I thought
Velcro was the height of technology at the time, and clearly those

super great. If you guys are reading this then "Hello!" from this new
life!

were the shoes of the future. Someday everybody would be wearing them, and frankly there was no reason to learn how to tie shoes.

I remember my dad and stepmom being frustrated because I didn't really learn how to tie my shoes until some years after this picture was taken. I finally learned more out of embarrassment than necessity. Much of my education in body presentation came this way.

Things were more complicated for Naomi in the style arena since she was older and cared more about her appearance than I did. She cared more about everything than I did, frankly. Our mother was never taught much about self-care (her own childhood marred by more extreme abuse and neglect), so she had no wisdom to share with Naomi. But Naomi never gave up hope that she could get it right. Every time she went to school excited about an outfit and came home crying after being bullied, I vowed to never care that much about the way I looked. Seemed like a whole lot of suffering for very little reward. The nineties grunge-era style arrived and it was kind of a godsend for us. Baggy ill-fitting clothes? Don't mind if I do.

So aside from wanting to make my father love me and think I was smart enough to tie my own shoes, as a kid I didn't pay much attention to what others thought of my clothes. And then I got to middle school (cue the horror film sound track).

TALK MORE, SMILE MORE

Middle school was a different world. The kids in my class started showing up with lunch *money* instead of lunch bags. Kids were showing up in outfits from a place called "the Gap" and wearing makeup and talking about bands and brands. I never listened to

music, didn't own any CDs. I hated getting dressed, but I couldn't wear an outfit for a week at a time anymore, because now people would gossip. I still didn't brush my hair, but nobody ever teased me about that. I may not have had lunch money or good hygiene or nice clothes, but I began to realize that I had something else: I was funny. It didn't matter how I looked or how I dressed as long as I could make people laugh. In sixth grade, a bully at school tried to get everyone to start calling me "pit stain" because of all the, well, yellow pit stains on my T-shirts. Once, when I was wearing one of my favorite shirts, he pointed out that he could "see my titties through my shirt." I replied blankly, "What titties? Oh. These aren't titties, I'm just fat." The whole class laughed because I was very obviously, and unabashedly, chubby and flat-chested. With the laughter from my classmates on my side, I proceeded to point out that the only reason he could see them was because he was so short.

That was the first and last time I was bullied in middle school. It was also the first and last time I bullied anybody else. Humiliating that kid in class didn't make me feel any better. It didn't feel good at all. I liked making people smile, and I didn't like seeing the hateful/hurtful look in his eyes when he knew I had bested him. I would rather have made him laugh, too.

But let's get back to clothing. I had narrowly escaped being labeled "pit stain," and suddenly I was well liked by my classmates and no one teased me about my appearance. I had a core group of friends, and at the center was my best friend, Rachel. All the families in Burlingame were well off, but Rachel's was *very* well off. And everybody knew it. From the outside, I'm sure we seemed like the Odd Couple, but the truth was that we had a very deep bond. We gave each other so much in terms of love and companionship. Rachel's family was incredibly generous, and Rachel's mother, Jane, was especially compassionate to my situation. She was a beautiful woman both inside and out. She'd had a tough childhood herself and had worked her way through it to be the woman she is today. It was inspiring, really. Her daughter was inspiring, too. I was kind of in love with the whole family.

With thick, dark hair, pale skin, and strong (these days people say "fierce") eyebrows over piercing green eyes, Rachel was the prettiest girl in whatever room we were in. There was something powerful and passionate about her. I "wasn't gay" at the time, but boy, was I supergay at the time.

The first time I went over to Rachel's house, my mom dropped me off and commented on what a beautiful home it was. She loved the manicured lawn out front. The way the flower pots framed the door. "These are the type of people we belong with," she said. When I rang the bell and heard the melody that chimed, I was in awe. Even the entryway sang songs of your arrival. This was the pinnacle of life. Rachel's house was big and smelled like a fancy store. It reminded me of walking into a Nordstrom or a Macy's, where everything was cool and clean and hinted of perfume. But it was cozier than a store. It was a home. With two stories and carpets. Rachel and some of our other friends answered the door. She was excited to show me her room and mentioned that before going upstairs I had to take off my shoes. My stomach dropped.

If underwear was hard to come by in my house, socks were scarcity itself.

The socks we did have were so overworn that they held the shape of your foot when you took them off, hardened at the toe, stained, and smelly. I really didn't want to take off my shoes, but Rachel's room was upstairs, and the second floor was covered in a pristine white carpet. So there wasn't much of a choice.

I took off my shoes last and tried to lag behind as much as possible as our group walked up the stairs to Rachel's room. I made it to the bedroom without incident, and as we sat on the floor, I positioned myself to hide my socks from view. Why I kept them on is beyond me. I really should have just taken them off and stuffed them into the soles of my shoes.

"Rachel!" Jane called from the stairwell.

"Yeah?" Rachel called back.

"Come here please!"

Rachel rolled her eyes and got up and went to talk to her mom. I followed because, well, probably because I didn't have the social graces to know that she was supposed to be talking to her mother alone. I was kind of like a puppy.

Jane was kneeling on the floor pointing to brown smears that were tracked on the freshly cleaned carpet.

"Honey, who wore their shoes upstairs?"

"Nobody!" Rachel was exasperated. She was a good daughter and knew the rules.

"Well, then, where did these come from?" she asked, pointing to the stains.

"I don't know! Maybe it was Minnie." Minnie was the family Maltese.

Jane looked as if she wasn't buying it, and I don't think Rachel knew the truth, but I did.

"I think that it was my socks," I spoke up and pointed to my feet. Jane looked up at me and then down at my feet and laughed. It wasn't unkind, it was more like an exasperated, suddenly sympathizing laugh. We all stared at my two mismatched, once white socks with a tiny pinky toe barely showing to one side.

"Okay, you take those off, those are filthy. We'll just throw them away, and Rachel can give you some socks." Jane was smiling.

I bent down to take them off, and Rachel said "I can clean the carpet!" but I insisted that I could clean it, too. Rachel said we would clean it together. From that point on, we really did everything together.

Rachel's family did their best to help me out with anything I needed, from food to school supplies. Rachel and I had such an organic and immediate friendship that it never felt like charity to me. It felt natural. And of course, years later, I would end up living with them as I finished high school. They were all impeccably dressed and well manicured, and they offered to help me with those things, too. But I didn't want to learn to do my own makeup—because I loved it when Rachel did my makeup for me. I'd sit on the sink in her bathroom, and she'd stand between my legs and gently paint my eyes and face. She'd line my lips and tell me to look up or down or to the side, and there wasn't anything I wouldn't do for her in those moments. She wasn't typically an affectionate friend, so that was the most we'd ever touch. And when she was done, she would tell me I was pretty.

Why would I ever learn to do my own makeup?

WAXING AND WANING

Middle school turned into high school, and high school for me was the dawn of my adulthood's battle against body hair. Our mother never told us to shave our legs, instead insisting that if we never did we'd never grow dark hairs. This was true for her perhaps, always a woman with fine hair and barely visible brows, but for Naomi and I our situation was the opposite. Our father's Jewish roots were embedded deep under our skin and were sprouting up with ferocious tenacity: thick black hairs that seemed to contradict the fairness of our eyes and face. Once, when I was talking to Naomi about the sheer volume of hair I was producing, she suggested that it was because I had too much testosterone and maybe I would need to get my hormones checked. "After all, you're really strong and you've basically got a beard."

Rachel suggested I get a bikini wax and I tried it once. The results being an acne-like rash that covered my thighs and crotch for many, many weeks. Increasingly socially uncomfortable with my body (and now itchy, too) I avoided all situations involving pools and shorts. My skin just couldn't take it.

In terms of clothing, high school was confusing for me because I wanted to feel confident and sexy, but didn't really get anything out of the attention I was receiving from the boys around me. Nothing from them felt the same as Rachel looking me over and saying, "That looks good. You're pretty."

Things continued to confuse me even after I accepted my sexuality in college. Now I understood what kind of person I was trying to attract, but had no idea how I was supposed to attract them. As a budding baby gay I didn't understand where I should fall on the spectrum.

Was I more butch or femme? I tried to look at the lesbians around me to figure it out. At the start of college I was pretty much a blob of acne and hair that I stuck under a beanie 99 percent of the time. Only after I started dating my first girlfriend did I try to tidy things up a bit. But whenever I put on makeup it would make her uncomfortable. And her discomfort heightened my own discomfort. Already not confident in my ability to properly paint my face, I gave it up entirely.

So as I grew more confident in my gayness, I grew less confident in my femininity. In my mind, it was one or the other. I felt like I had to toe this line with all the women I dated, checking off boxes in my head as to which one of us was playing the role of the "man" and thus had to (literally) wear the pants.

Did I drive more often? Yes.

Did I pay for more meals? Yes.

Did I usually initiate sex? Yes.

Was I always doling out the orgasms? Yes.

Was I physically stronger? Yes.

Was I the bigger spoon? Yes.

For a while this was my simplistic, linear way of understanding gender roles within relationships.[4] Depending on how feminine the woman I dated was, I would adjust accordingly. Combine this with a propensity to "chase" straight women until they incited a sexual encounter, and sometimes I felt downright manly.

But then I would find myself wanting to wear makeup and heels. And look pretty. And feel pretty. Because I like being pretty dammit.

So what did I want? Was I a top or a bottom? What should I wear on my top and/or bottom? I'd always dated beautiful women, but what if I wanted to be a beautiful woman, too? Would that mean I

---

4 Don't even get me started on trying to pick out a bathing suit.

would have to date a more masculine lesbian to find someone who was interested in me? What was I looking for?

Around age twenty-six I started to realize that I really wanted both. I wanted to be a beautiful woman dating a beautiful woman who wanted to fuck me. A bad-ass boss who thought I looked cute in a snapback hat but also cute without it. Someone who loved me and the diversity within me.

The better I understood myself and who I was, the better I understood what I wanted my outer style to reflect. I spent years looking at myself through the eyes of other people: overthinking how much mascara to put on before a date by studying what types of pics the girl I'm courting likes on my Instagram. Does she like the pics of me in full hair and makeup? Or is she a fan of the clean look?

But as I get older I'm letting go of the hetero-normative idea that being in a relationship has to mean adhering to traditional gender roles. For me, feeling sexy isn't about a short skirt or a fitted shirt. It's about feeling in control of the confines of my clothing. Revealing exactly as much or as little of myself as I want.

What I can see now is that my relationship with my body has been dictated by resistance. Deep down, I always cared about the way I looked, but I wouldn't allow myself to accept that fact because I'd come to believe that caring meant humiliation or admitting a lack of resource or understanding. Part of me would like to end this chapter with a lovely little message along the lines of "True beauty comes from within" or "The opinions of others don't matter." Those are both fair and decent messages that I'd like you to consider and embrace in your own time. But what I've discovered is this:

It's not superficial to care about the way you look. There's nothing wrong with enjoying the time spent on your appearance if that's part of your self-care. People may use labels such as "vain" or "shallow" to try and keep you in a box, to make you feel small. But those people are usually just insecure themselves. Nobody else gets to tell you what you should or should not care about in terms of your looks. That's something you get to decide all for yourself. If you want to shave[5] off all your pubes, that doesn't make you antifeminist. If you like to work out because you want killer abs for the summer, go for it—but that doesn't mean anyone else has to.

With our bodies we make statements before we speak, our presentation is a language spoken without words. You—and only you—get to decide what it is you're trying to say.

---

5   I had considered making this chapter about the first time I got laser hair removal. My friend Erica gifted me a coupon after graduation from college and I've been a huge advocate ever since. Let me just sum up that story by saying this: unexpected lasering of the butthole with surprisingly effective results!

HOCUS FOCUS

I hate to admit this because I like to think I'm very cool and calm and collected and cocky and confident and blah blah blah but the fact of the matter is, I'm just not.

For instance when I'm into a girl, I immediately start to panic. I overthink every text, every conversation, every interaction, no matter how small or how basic. There is no playing hard to get for me. I just can't do it. Instead, when I like someone, I want things to happen at warp speed. If there is someone I want to get to know, I want to get to know that person right away, superquick, all at once, now or never! All or nothing. That's my thought spiral. You're in or you're out. You win or you die. *Game of Thrones* is the best. Etc., etc., etc.

The truth is, I repeat this pattern in *all* areas of my life, not just in dating but literally in everything I do. I just can't slow down, I can't play it cool, I can't stay in the frame. Long story short, I didn't have a grip on my focus, my focus had its grips on me.

In early 2013 I was feeling incredibly overwhelmed. From January to March of that year, all of my big projects and ideas were greenlit at once. In January I got my first book deal; in February I launched the campaign for the *Hello, Harto!* Tour; and in March my friends and I made our first film *Camp Takota*, that we would start filming in August. (Right around the same time as the manuscript deadline for my book, only two weeks after getting back from tour.) Oh, and during all of this I also needed to post two videos a week to the channel. My time was limited and needed to be managed and managed well. I could get it all done so long as I could just stay focused. Which . . . well . . . you know. Wasn't my forte.

In the midst of all this chaos I was in my first adult relationship. I had been dating my girlfriend, Francesca, for about six months when I told her I thought I needed to see a psychiatrist. I'd been seeing a therapist for almost two years at that point, but I felt I wasn't making progress. I felt as though there were certain patterns that my brain had decided for me and that all the talk wasn't really helping. Good days and bad days felt as though they were totally outside of my control; good days being days when I got a lot done and took good care of myself, bad days being when I'd spend the day pacing the floor, trying to figure out what to do next.

Worst of all, there was simply no room for a bad day. This was my big year of opportunity, the reason for all the risks I had taken. But with so many irons in the fire, I constantly felt as if I were one false move away from burning the whole house down. Which would send me on a spiral which would lead to another bad day and so on and so forth.

Despite all of this, part of me genuinely believed I could do it all. Because I usually thrived on pressure. In college, I started all of my papers the night before they were due, and I never outlined. My se-

nior thesis (which was a comparative analysis of memory and auto-
biography!) was written over the course of one panicked day. I never
wrote first drafts, everything left the printer as final. I never learned
structure or systems to do things differently because up until that
point the pressure had worked for me.

Until 2013.

Suddenly I had so much going on that flying by the seat of my
pants just wasn't going to work anymore. I needed to learn to be more
organized and to create deadlines for myself.

My therapist had helped me in many ways, but some days (due
to the level of shit I was processing) sessions with her left me feeling
vulnerable and drained and sad—and that was not a good state to be
in when later that day I had to get drunk and cook.

I tried exercise as a way of managing my anxiety—walking
had always helped me clear my head and was usually a good way to
reset my system. That helped, but I couldn't pick which direction I
needed to be pointed in since all my obligations were equally urgent
and equally important. And since I was used to getting 100% done at
once, these larger products[1] that would require multiple drafts and
edits and attempts, were my nightmare. I didn't know how to do
things 10–50% at a time. So instead I stayed trapped at 0% checking
one project off at a time.

Hard to prioritize when everything feels like a priority.

Other things I tried: caffeine (which was great! but it made
me sleepless and anxious), meditation (which helps me a lot today, but at that point I couldn't do it *at all*), and lots and lots of anger and stressing out and feeling like a hopeless failure who was

---

1   You can't write a 200+-page book in one sitting. You can't plan a 10-week
    tour in one sitting. You can't film a 90-minute movie in one sitting.

a fool for even thinking I could handle things. Why couldn't I just focus and be present? Everyone around me seemed to be dealing just fine, so why couldn't I? Clearly, there was something wrong with me.

When I got home from the *Hello, Harto!* Tour, I was exhausted and depleted and facing the reality that I now had two weeks to write an entire book before moving into production on our film. I had overextended myself and was an absolute emotional wreck.

I voiced all of this to Francesca, who was supportive; she loved me and was probably also eager to find out if there was anything to be done about my obsessive thought spirals that seemed to appear out of nowhere and consume me completely.

Eventually I went to see a psychiatrist my therapist had recommended whose office was on the other side of LA. The traffic getting there was exceptional, and didn't help my anxiety about the appointment. My thoughts were in a loop:

What if this is how schizophrenia starts? What if that's what she tells me, "Hannah, you're just like your mom, and you're inventing all of these worries. You're going to need to spend weeks in a hospital to sort out your brain." Oh God, I really don't have time for that.

What if I'm somehow both depressed AND debilitatingly anxious? What if she needs to put me on a rotation of antidepressants during the day and antianxiety meds throughout the night? What if the meds don't work? What if it takes six weeks before we even know if they're the right medications to begin with? Oh God, I don't have time for that either.

Wait . . . what if . . . what if the drugs make me content but . . . I lose the ability to be funny?

I don't know which of those thoughts scared me more, the idea of having a debilitating illness or the idea that taking medication might make me less funny. This whole medication thing was starting to feel like a lose-lose. Why was I even going to this appointment?

"So what brings you here today?"

Oh. The appointment was starting.

I had been so lost in my head that I had somehow parked the car, entered the building, gone up in the elevator, and checked into the appointment on autopilot. Now I was sitting across from an older woman who reminded me slightly of Professor Umbridge from Harry Potter.

"Um. I'm just here. I guess."

She smiled, eased back in her chair, and began to explain how the session would work.

"First I'd like to outline my insurance policy, I don't take insurance, but I can provide you with documentation that shows—"

The woman spoke at a turtle's pace! I was trying to be on my best behavior, sitting still and listening. She was so methodical and deliberate in her speech. I wondered if she was a Jehovah's Witness. That's the thing, you know. You never can tell. But wait, there was a cross on her desk. Definitely not a Witness. They believe that crosses are "idolatry." How bonkers.

"Does that sound fair to you?"

"Absolutely, yes." During my thought parade she had mapped out her billing system in detail. I wasn't listening, but I heard what she said.

"So I'm going to start by asking you some questions."

"Okay!"

She proceeded to ask a series of questions about my family history—mental health and emotional stuff—along with questions about my daily routine, my career, my stresses, my joys, and so on. There was a clock on the wall behind her, and I wondered if she put it there so that clients would be aware of how long the session was lasting.

Another thing I noticed while she was asking her questions was that she kept shifting between four sheets of paper. She had them in her lap against a leather file folder and after I answered each question she would make notes on the different pages. At first she wrote on all four, and then eventually shifted to writing back and forth on the same two sheets. Eventually she was writing her notes down only on one sheet. I looked at the clock to see how far we'd come in the session, we were nearing the end of the first hour. Why was this thing two hours long anyway? What was going to happen in the second hour?

She cleared her throat and I glanced away from the clock back at her face. She looked down and seemed to assume a more casual air when she asked:

"As a child, did you ever have difficulty in the classroom?"

Oh, my god. She thinks I have ADD.

"You think I have ADD."

My tone was curt. I was frustrated, and I didn't want to keep dancing around with her.

She didn't seem surprised by my curtness. Almost as if she had expected it, she replied, "Is that something *you've* heard before?"

"Well, yeah, I mean . . . like from my teachers and stuff."

She was taking notes again. "Do you know what years?"

"Like what grades? I dunno. Like in second grade . . . I remember we had a school assessment test and I was only supposed to complete it up to a certain point in the packet, but I didn't know that, so I completed the whole packet and turned it in. I always turned my test in first, by the way. Not that I was always getting an A, but I always got through tests really fast. I don't know if that's relevant, but I thought I'd share. Anyway, I finished the whole packet, which went up to the fifth-grade level, and then the teacher wanted to have a special meeting about it because apparently I had done really good. They wanted to put me into the GATE program, which was for gifted kids, so that was really cool."

"Did you go into that program?"

"GATE? No. We couldn't afford it. Actually, my mom never even made it to the meeting. She was proud of me, though."

"I see." She smiled. It felt a little condescending. "Now back to my question, did any of your teachers ever tell you that you might have ADHD?"

"ADHD? What's that? Is that the same as ADD?"

"ADD is becoming an outdated term. It doesn't include the intensity of focus—the hyperfocus—that is also part of the diagnosis. In my practice, I believe that ADHD is the more appropriate assessment."

"Huh. That's cool. I didn't know that." I was fully tuned in to our session now. ADHD was a term I hadn't heard before. I wanted to know more. This was getting interesting.

She was quiet. I was quiet. Oh she was waiting for me to continue answering her question. Right.

"Okay, lemme think. In second grade, they did say to my mom that they thought I had ADD . . . or ADHD . . . did they call it that then? Sorry, doesn't matter. Then there was something in fifth grade, and then again in eighth, and then, yeah, my sophomore year in high school my math teacher wanted me to see somebody. Because I never did any of the homework, but I did well on the tests. I loved to participate in class, but outside of the classroom I just kind of . . . lost focus."

"So you operate well with structure?"

"I guess it's more like—" I had to stop and think. "I guess it's more like I operate well under pressure."

"Perhaps you've used pressure because you've lacked the ability to create your own structure."

"I never thought of that."

"Most people with ADHD don't realize that. Through years of failing to perform, though sometimes excelling despite this, they feel a constant state of underachievement."

"Yeah!" I was excited. "Man, I just always feel like I have all these great ideas and things I want to do, but I just don't do them! I just can't do them! I totally feel that way. I've basically done nothing with my life."

She smiled, and this time it seemed kind. "Given that you have two degrees, are responsible for the financial support of your family, and also on an upward trajectory in your career—I'd have to disagree with that assessment."

I was quiet. It didn't feel right to accept her praise, but I didn't have any way to refuse it except to say, "Thanks, but it doesn't feel like accomplishment to me."

"Does anything?"

The clock on the wall showed that we had only ten minutes left. I was hoping to get out of this with a prescription in my hand, so I pushed past her question in an effort to save time. I didn't want to spend another $400 for two hours of talking.

"So what do I do?" I asked.

"First I'd like you to read a book called *Driven to Distraction*. It's very well written, and written for the adult ADHD mind. It has a series of case studies from successful people who late in life found themselves sitting in rooms like this one, expressing that same sense of failure and emotional disregulation."

"Is that what I'm doing? Haha. Okay. I'll get that book. Anything else?"

"I'd also like to give you a prescription for Adderall. Ten milligrams. Take half a pill a day, and see how it makes you feel and for how long. It's a medication that acts instantly, so if you have a negative reaction, don't panic because it will leave your system within a few hours."

That sounded scary. "What kind of reaction?"

"Adderall is a stimulant, so some find that it makes them . . . more agitated. Fidgety."

"MORE fidgety than I already am?? Ha! I don't want that!"

She was writing on her prescription pad. "I don't think you'll have that reaction. Stimulants focus the mind with ADHD. I'm anticipating that you'll be just fine."

"Like having a cup of coffee and taking a nap."

"I'm not sure I follow."

"It's like how sometimes you have a cup of coffee and it like . . . wakes you up enough for you to realize you're sleepy. So then you go and take a nap."

She laughed. For the first time in the session. It felt nice. Like I could finally relax.

"Well, that's an interesting analogy . . . We're out of time. Let's book an appointment for next week and check in then."

"Okay. Thank you." I stood and shook her hand. It was an exciting thought, that maybe my thoughts could be more contained. That maybe I did need a little help and that it was okay to accept it.

I went on the Adderall long enough for her to confirm that my ADHD was real (because it made me sit still instead of bouncing off the walls), but it was really difficult for me to take a pill several times a day. I had been raised with an incredible stigma about doctors and medication, and popping pills to be "normal" was hard to accept. I told my doctor, and she switched me to an extended-release medication called Vyvanse.

Vyvanse sucked. It blunted me emotionally and hurt my kidneys and was just not good. I wasn't excited, I wasn't motivated. I was just . . . flat.

So I went back on the Adderall with less judgment. Finding the right dose took time, but eventually I got into a rhythm that I could sustain.

But what was even more helpful was the book. *Driven to Distraction* changed the way I viewed my brain and my life. It showed that my brain wasn't broken, and that brought me great relief. It was just a brain that didn't do very well in our current education and employment structures. But it wasn't my brain's fault.

And I think that thought, "This is all my fault" or "I'm just being weak," keeps people from talking to therapists or psychiatrists to get the support they need.

But it's not weakness. It's strength.

It takes strength to allow yourself to seek help. To seek allies. To get the support you need. It's like adding a quiver to your bow. If you were taking aim at the goals in your life, you'd stand there and fire as many arrows as it took to meet them, right? And what if you realized that the arrows you were firing sometimes broke apart midflight and went all sorts of directions? You'd wish you just send them in one, right? That's the way I like to think about getting the help I need for my ADHD.

If you feel as if your own arrows are misfiring or that life has given you only so many arrows, remember that change is possible but will take time. Remember we all process at different speeds. It's neither 0% nor 100% .

NO JUDGING

I survived the environment I grew up in by training my brain to function by "surviving," a state of extreme awareness in which I was constantly inputting information and making judgments to protect myself and my loved ones. But as I grew older and entered the "thriving" stage of my life, I encountered a problem: the habit of hyperawareness followed me, and I became, well, very judgmental.

There is a lot of judgment in the world around us. The Internet is a place that's full of judgment because the Internet is full of people. People who, from one computer to the next, spend their time commenting on and communicating with and judging other humans. The Internet can also be a wonderful place to meet people. I'm glad to have lived through the dawn of online dating, watching as the stigma of meeting your partner through a website or an app has slowly faded away. And I've met some great people because of the Internet—in particular, my friend Grace Helbig.

You know how sometimes you meet someone and you become

friends almost instantly? Like the connection is so raw and organic, it's as if you've already known each other for a lifetime? Like the two of you are speaking a secret language and you suddenly feel so blessed to have someone in your life who *gets you*?

That's not how it was with me and Grace.

Grace and I were first introduced when I was living in New York. Her friend Michelle (another online content creator) had reached out to me and asked if I wanted to get dinner with the two of them. There weren't many other YouTubers in New York at the time, so I gladly accepted the invitation.

From what I remember of that dinner, we ate at a French restaurant on Park and 20th, and Michelle did most of the talking. Grace was quiet. Tall, blond, pretty, and honestly kind of shy. I remember being surprised because I would have thought that someone who looked like her would have had natural confidence. Instead, here was this smart and quietly funny person with poor posture who clearly let the alpha in the conversation lead. She was a beta. Or so it seemed.

As the dinner drew to a close, I felt decidedly "meh" about Grace. And I felt that my judgment was final. My attitude was, if someone isn't going to make the effort to draw me in, then I'm not going to be bothered with drawing them out. If you had told me that this person would eventually become one of my closest friends and business partners, I wouldn't have believed you. If you had told me that this person and I would go on to have some of the most cataclysmic fights I've ever had in friendships, I would not have believed you. If you had told me that one night I'd drive this person to a hospital to get stitches in her forehead because she'd fallen down some stairs, I wouldn't have believed you. And if you had told me that another night we'd play Carnegie Hall together, only to find ourselves laughing so hard we cried after one of us (Grace) peed on the other's favorite hat, I would have listened politely and then muttered an excuse as I walked away from our conversation.

But that's the thing about judgment. If you give your initial opinion of someone too much weight and accept it as fact before really taking the time to really get to know someone, you risk missing out on a lot. I'm glad I didn't let that happen with Grace. I was wrong about her when we first met. I never expected that the shy girl across from me at the dinner table would become one of my favorite people to turn to for advice or for a lively debate. I never thought that this seeming "beta" of a babe would turn out to be one of the most open-minded and supportive people I know when it came to listening to opposing ideas. Today our friendship is categorized by periods of extreme work, extreme play, and extreme understanding. Understanding is incredibly important in a friendship. Grace is probably the person in my life I am most comfortable admitting my mistakes to.

Good thing, since Grace and I have made more than our fair share of mistakes together.

Grace and I had been filming together in Vancouver for five weeks. The project was *Electra Woman and Dyna Girl: Rebooted!*, a modern remake of a series from the 1970s that no one has ever heard of. Well, I shouldn't say no one, but whenever someone has heard of it, I'm surprised. My literary agent, Jodi, for instance, is a fan of the series and was excited to hear that the remake was happening and that the story had been given a modern twist. The original series involved spandex, go-go boots, and the generally accepted sexism that was common for the era. But Grace and I were determined that our reboot wouldn't involve any of those things. We eventually won our battle, but only after holding the project up for two days as we rewrote scripts until 4 a.m.

Shooting the series was an ambitious project: fourteen-hour days, week after week, learning stunts, memorizing scripts that were only just finalized, and finally maintaining each of our separate businesses while operating out of Canada for six weeks. But Grace and I share an intense work ethic: we both like to muscle through projects no matter the cost. Health? Pfft. Mental wellness? Pfft. If we can walk away, we're fine.[1]

During our final weekend of filming, Grace and I had a lot of steam we needed to let off. Which is how I explain the events that occurred on the Night of the Tattoos.

Before I get into what happened, I should tell you that Grace had no tattoos before that night, but I had gotten my first tattoo when I was twenty-four. That was back when I was going through a period of intense depression and would spend all day lying on my friend's couch staring at the ceiling. It was just after I had moved to New York for a fresh start in a new city. (But I could not find the drive to make the most of the opportunity. I had plenty of ambition, I just had no ammunition. It was as if I could see my target, I held my gun, but I had no desire to pull the trigger.)

In those days I could talk about the things I wanted to do, and that would excite me; I could work alongside a friend and feed off her motivation, but when left to my own devices, I just couldn't put my money where my mouth was. For instance, at the time, I wanted to try to write a novel. I could see the ideas in my head, outlines even!

---

1 I'm happy to say that that phase is coming to a close and we're both much more balanced now, blessedly.

I had a laptop and I lived in Brooklyn, where coffee shops were in abundance. I had everything I needed, but every morning when I woke up, it just seemed easier to stay in bed and daydream rather than to live my dream. In order for that pattern of behavior to change, I decided I needed to get a tattoo.

My thinking was not that if I got a tattoo it would be the answer to all my problems. Rather, it would serve as a symbol to remind me that I was in control of my own desires and could make things happen. I wanted to put a symbol on my chest that would remind me to get up and start the motions. At first I thought it would be a rhythm symbol or a bass clef, something music-related to keep tempo with my temperament. But I wasn't a musician, and besides having a strong affinity for music, I couldn't claim that any of those symbols would hold any deep significance for me.

What symbols were important to me? The symbol of the cross crossed my mind—freshman year of college, I'd worn a silver cross around my neck and lived in the straight-edge dorms (meaning no drugs or alcohol allowed). That was also my final year of repressing/denying my homosexuality.

Clearly a cross wouldn't do. I spent many a couch-ridden morning contemplating the decision. I realized that I didn't want a symbol from my past; I wanted something that signified my future and would give me the motivation to start moving in the right direction. Then one day it came to me: a play button! I wanted to put the movie of my life into motion. I wanted to start making things happen. A play button would be perfect! Something I could push as many times as I needed to. Something that would set things back into motion, no matter how hard it was for me to get off the couch.

However, being the balanced and even-natured person that I am (not), I thought I might drive myself insane with the constant expectation of activity. So naturally, I decided I needed a pause button, too.

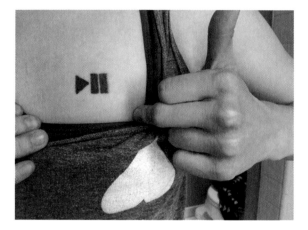

Before making that lifelong commitment, I did my research on the best tattoo shops in town. I realized that it wasn't going to be the most intricate piece of art, but I'm a bit of a hypochondriac and I wanted to get it done in a place that was clean, classy, and safe. After about a month of deliberation (even going so far as to draw the symbol on my chest to make sure I liked it), I finally went to a tattoo shop on Smith Street in Brooklyn to get a consultation. About a week after that, I went in for the tattoo. It was a cool, controlled, and calm experience that was a definite marker in my life. I felt proud and rational and free of any doubt that I had made a good decision.

Getting my second tattoo with Grace, however, was the opposite sort of experience.

On the Night of the Tattoos, Grace and I were both in conflict with our significant others. Grace's conflicts with her boyfriend were always very loud and passionate, as is the nature of their relationship. My girlfriend, Francesca, and I were also in conflict, but the kind of conflict that's quiet—the quiet of two people who know that something is about to go terribly wrong. The quiet before an earthquake. Except who knew if the earthquake was going to bring forth a volcano and who knew if that volcano would destroy everything we had built. Francesca and I had said our quiet, conflicted good nights, and Grace's boyfriend had booked an early flight from Canada as a spontaneous act to prove a point in an argument with her.

As I said, it had been a bit of a rough trip.

So the evening found us decompressing over bottles of white wine and Motown music in the hotel-apartments we stayed in during the shoot. We made kale chips and were lying around commiserating about romance while steadily getting more and more drunk. We may have had a little more wine than was good for us, but I will give us this: we have always been very good at looking at each other's relationships objectively while being completely subjective about our own. It's so easy to talk through those conflicts because we've never had the added pressure of being in love with each other.

Oh, maybe I should say something about that.

As a giant, raging lesbian, I can say without a shadow of a doubt that I've never had a crush on Grace Helbig. Isn't that wild? I mean, it's pretty natural to assume that after all these years I'd be secretly in love with her. And trust me, I'd tell you if it was true! Or at least I'd try to cleverly allude to the fact that I was—but I'm not. Maybe it's because she's a Libra and I'm a Scorpio. Maybe it's because we've always just been buds. We've been drunk together many times, and we've never once made out! Isn't that nuts? And we're both the type of people who love to make out when drunk. Grace's explanation for it would be that she's straight, but I have plenty of friends who are "straight" who I've smooched! Grace has always been like a sister to me. Like Naomi. Unfortunately for Grace and Naomi, I can be a bit of a bully sometimes, which leads me back to how we ended up getting those tattoos.

Despite the fact that both of our relationships roughly resembled cyclones, my (drunken) sense was that we were actually both pretty grounded. I was expressing that to Grace when it hit me: this was exactly what my next tattoo should be about: groundedness! I wanted something that would remind me to stay grounded. Grounded in fame. Grounded in my expectations. Grounded in what was important to me. And I needed the tattoo now. I immediately started googling symbols for staying grounded and decided on the alchemy symbol for "earth"—perfect! I like geometric shapes, and, frankly, I was being drunk and impulsive.

I showed the symbol to Grace, and she agreed. "Okay, then, let's do it!" She was sitting on the floor with her back against the couch. I was lying by her feet idly examining her toes.

"Yeah? Okay, yeah! But I don't think anything will be open at this hour." I searched on my phone for "Vancouver Tattoo shops that are open right now." Naturally, since it was 11:30 p.m., nothing turned up.

"Oh, come on, there has to be *something*. Here, let me call the concierge and see if they know."

"No, dude, tattoo shops aren't like that. They are real shops, and they close at seven or something!" Despite saying that, I had decided to start calling random numbers of tattoo shops I'd found on my phone to see if, by some miracle, someone might pick up.

Both our searches were in vain—although while calling the concierge Grace had managed to order herself another martini and me a vodka soda—and we were very close to giving up. That's when my phone rang.

"Hello?"

"Did you just kick the door?" The man on the line sounded very bothered.

"Excuse me?"

"Who is this?"

"Uh—Hannah?"

"What do you want?"

"Nothing—oh! Wait! Sorry, but do you do tattoos?"

"Yeah, I do. That's why I asked if you were just trying to kick down my door."

The conversation was confusing. But then again, I was drunk, so everything was oscillating between being extremely clear and extremely vague.

"No. We are at our hotel. I'm not kicking your door. Look, I'm just trying to get a tattoo done before I leave town tomorrow." A lie, but I wanted to create a sense of urgency to justify the late-night call. "And I'm just hoping you will do it. It's a simple geometric thing. Won't take long."

"I've closed my shop. Sorry, but I—"

"What if I paid you a *stupid* amount of money? Like double the cost of what you normally charge."

"For what exactly?"

"A triangle. With a line through it," I said, describing the symbol of earth.

"And you would pay me—"

"Double whatever your standard rate is." At that point I could sense him coming around, and I needed to be incredibly confident in my decision. Despite its spontaneity. Despite the hour of night. Despite the ridiculous amount of money I was willing to pay.

"I'd have to reopen the shop. I can do it, but it's gonna be around 1 a.m. What do you think about that?"

"Perfect. Great. We will see you there at one."

"We?"

"My friend is coming, too."

"Okay, but no funny business. I need to pick up my wife." He sounded anxious and angry.

"Um . . . yeah. Anyway, thanks. See you then."

Our conversation ended, and I won't say that it left me with the best feeling in the world, but I certainly wasn't going to let that show. Not to my dear friend Grace, who was already biting her nails and looking around as though she wanted to change her mind.

"He's in. Are you changing your mind? We don't have to do this."

"NO! I'm totally down. I mean, if you're sure."

"Sure, I'm sure." I wasn't sure. But whatever. Let's do this.

"Great. So let's go."

"Well, it won't be for another hour. Also, it's gonna be a bit of a cab ride."

"Did he sound sketchy?"

Grace was standing now and couldn't stop checking her phone. I knew she was feeling uncertain about the plan but I chose to ignore the physical signs of her discomfort, because if she didn't come, I wasn't going to go. So I needed her to come with me. Especially now that our drinks had just arrived.

"It's Canada, so how sketchy could it be?"

To say the place was sketchy would be an understatement. Without going into too much detail, I'll do my best to describe the experience as I remember it.

* The shop owner was an old, fat man with buggy eyes who said he was a psychic and immediately told Grace that she had irritable bowels and an anxiety disorder. He was not really interested in me.

* His "wife" was there. She looked to be about twenty-three years old and was cleaning instruments at a sink in the front. She was silent and unhappy.

* There was also a young man in the back cleaning the shop owner's gun collection. Why he was there at 1 a.m., I'll never know. HE WAS LITERALLY CLEANING MACHINE GUNS. Well, maybe not machine guns, but they looked scary. He cleaned in silence, perfectly content to pay us no mind and to focus on cleaning these guns.

* Halfway through the process, the Child Bride (as we very crassly dubbed her in later conversation) came in and said to the shop owner, "Someone threw a brick at your Smart car." That made him very angry. She continued, "They smashed your front window." That made him even angrier. He stopped what he was doing to go outside and look. There was only a crack in the windshield, thankfully, but it gave him no peace.

* I tried to diffuse the tension in the room by saying that it could have been an accident. He refused to acknowledge this statement.

* Grace tried to defuse the tension in the room by very bluntly pointing out "Hannah is getting an important

tattoo right now, so maybe we should talk about something more positive." She said that having just finished getting her tattoo and fiddling with the Saran Wrap around her ankle.

His response was to tell us the following: "Someone did it on purpose."

"Oh, I'm sure that's not true. It's not like you have enemies, right?"

"Well, no offense to you, but all women are attention seeking and there was a group of girls going around spreading lies about me. And I'm sure they did it. I'm sure they were the ones who were kicking at the door earlier, too."

Yes, it was very sketchy. And very icky. So sketchy and icky that we rode home in the cab feeling totally sober. And probably a little shell-shocked.

Despite how weird the night was and how uncomfortable we felt, I can say with full confidence that I never actually felt unsafe. Although I often fall prey to my impulses, I trust my instincts. And there was no prickly feeling on the back of my neck, no drop in the pit of my stomach. The situation was weird, to be sure, but I never for a second got the feeling that we needed to run. If you do ever get that feeling, I would say run. Always run.

When I awoke the next morning, I saw that the tattoo seemed clean and well done. We had gotten home safely and had each retired to her room to get some sleep. Thus, upon waking, I felt calm.

For about five minutes.

As the panic and doubt set in, I went straight to Grace's room. I needed to talk to her about the experience because there's nothing to be gained from running mental circles in solitude.

But first I went out and bought Saran Wrap and Polysporin for our tattoos because I certainly didn't want us getting infections.

When I entered the room, I threw myself onto Grace's bed and it all came pouring out. I was in a spiral, full tilt: *I'm so sorry. Did I make us do this? Why am I like this? How was this grounded? How could I make a decision like this when we were drinking? Am I a bad person? Did I put us in danger? Am I a bad friend? When will I stop being so impulsive? I'm so sorry if I put us in danger. If you hate your tattoo, I totally understand.*

In her gentle-giant sort of way, Grace talked me down by saying that I was not an impulsive *person*, I had just done an impulsive *thing*. And maybe I needed to be a little bit reckless to remind myself to stay grounded. Grace's reaction calmed me, and she was right. Now every time I look at my tattoo it reminds me of a night that could have gone *badly*. And that I could stand to be a little more patient, to take a little more time before making a decision, and to think things through before committing. *Grounded.*

When Grace finished her explanation, she asked me if I wanted to order room service and watch *Real Housewives* for a bit. I tucked myself under the covers and gratefully accepted.

I've always had the tendency to think of my relationships (platonic, romantic, and so on) as either zero or one hundred, black or white, with nothing in between. But my friendship with Grace has helped me to see that there are shades of gray. That no one out there is either "flawed" or "flawless" and that it's as dangerous to think that someone is perfect as it is to think he or she is poison. Grace has taught me how to be more guarded when appropriate and how to practice patience before judging myself (or others) too harshly.

(pictured above, my sweet tatt)

FILM THIS MOMENT

As I write this, my fellow YouTubers Mamrie Hart, Grace Helbig, and I are on our way to what will be our bajillionth (or like twentieth) #NoFilterShow together. This time in Australia. The #NoFilterShow is a live comedy show that the three of us perform that includes a raucous opening song and dance, a bunch of puns, improv games with the audience, sketches, live fanfiction reenactments, and drinking. At this point we've performed in cities in Canada and all across the United States. Even a handful of shows in the United Kingdom! It all sounds so great, right?

But if you had asked me three years ago whether I would be happily boarding a sixteen-hour flight to Australia to perform in five different cities over the course of seven days only to land back home in the States on Christmas Eve, I would have laughed in your face. Not in a rude way. But in a "Are you kidding me? Hell no, live performance makes me feel physically ill" kind of way.

The first time I can remember "performing live" was in my fifth-grade talent show, which I happily hosted with a very sweet girl named Molly Choma. I have no recollection of the talent show itself, but I do remember standing on my tiptoes to reach the mic above the podium. My stage partner was already a head taller than me, and tall stage partners would go on to become a recurring theme in my life.

Aside from our height difference and the shiny/shellacked mahogany feel of the podium under my hand, the other memory that stands out from that day is the unencumbered joy I felt when the audience of parents and peers laughed as I went off script. My act was subconscious, the same "class clown" instinct that got me in trouble in my classes and caused giggles in my friends. When your mouth is saying something before your brain even processes it—sometimes it's funny, sometimes it's shitty—it's hard to know when you're going to need to bite your tongue when your tongue is doing all the decision making.[1]

I can't remember the exact jokes I told or how appropriate they were, but I know I loved the reaction they got. I loved making people laugh. I loved making people happy. Their happy was my happy, too.

That revelation didn't lead me directly into a life in performing. It wouldn't have been practical, but also the idea of it was slightly terrifying. I struggled with memorization, and the kids I knew who excelled at acting, singing, or dancing, all seemed so confident and brave.

The next time I stepped onstage was in eighth grade. Again, it was as the host of a school talent show. My class-clown instincts had followed me to middle school, and I was known by all as "the funny one." I loved being known for something, and being funny was something I could do naturally, spontaneously, and sporadically. No commitments. No consequences. Except for the occasional stern

---

1   College was a lot like that, too, but in a much . . . much gayer way.

words from a teacher after class or hurting a friend's feelings with a callous quip.[2]

This time, I was again called to the stage with much protestation and false humility. Of course I knew that I would be a good host. I just didn't want anyone to know, GOD FORBID, that I thought that much of myself. That was eighth grade, remember. Much cooler to be passive than passionate.

My partner for that show was one of my best friends and on-again-off-again "crush" Gavin. He was funny, cute, and a great actor. Our friendship would evolve into short bouts of dating, eventually culminating in a friendship that would lead to his family's adoption of my little sister Maggie. But that's another story entirely.

During the eighth-grade show, I again went off script, but that time for about ten minutes. There was a technical delay with one of the acts, and I was told to stall. To stall I went onstage and proceeded to share what was on my mind with the crowded room. I told the same stories and jokes I would tell to any of my friends, pretending that the large and darkened room was simply the kid I was sitting next to in class. I don't remember much of the set, but I do remember my last joke. To the best of my ability, I believe it went something like this:

And one last thing: why do teachers keep the tissues at the front of the class? I mean, I get it, it's easy for everyone to see where the tissues are. That's great! Nobody has to ask and interrupt! But at the front of the class? That means that any time you have to blow your nose, you have to walk in

---

2 Rare, but still. Sometimes funny people can be mean without knowing/ meaning it.

---

front of everyone to do it! [At that point I mimed a discreet walk to the front of a classroom, trying my best not to interrupt the lesson while also pretending to blow my nose loudly into the mic while casting a deer-in-headlights look at the group.]

The audience loved it, and I loved their love. I felt full and happy and present. It was like the feeling you get after you finish a great workout or a superexcellent orgasm. Blissful nonthought. Nothing but the moment. Total. Complete. Clarity.

There were weeks of praise that followed and teachers telling me I was destined for a career in stand-up. One teacher even told me about a hilarious comedian named Ellen she thought I would love.

I loved the attention, but I didn't let it go to my head. Even at that age, I sensed that I needed to pursue a more reliable career path. In high school, I worked on the newspaper and was the yearbook editor. I channeled my creative energy into writing: I wrote columns and creative essays for my classes and letters to myself.

In summers during high school, I worked. I had three local jobs: at the video store, at the ice cream shop, and as an amateur bookkeeper for Rachel's mom. My performing in those days was limited to singing in the shower—being a "theater kid" seemed self-indulgent. Self-indulgent sounds harsh. I mean self-indulgent for me. I think if I'd had the time or the guts, I would have tried to participate in performance stuff more, but it just wasn't in the cards at that moment.

However, I did host the talent show again in high school, this time trying to mask my fear and insecurity and lack of preparation by wearing a pair of high heels and a tight pleather skirt. Again it went well, again I improvised, again I was too scared to admit that I loved being a performer.

Today, as I write this on the plane, sitting next to Mamrie on the way to Australia, I think about how far I've come as a performer. And how much I've learned about working together from Grace and Mamrie. Mamrie in particular always "gives it to me straight." It's amazing to think about how much she's supported me, how much she's guided me—

—and how much she terrified me when we first met.

W hat if I go onstage and I just ask the audience for questions and give them my answers? Like lessons from an amateur adult."

"Yeah, but that's not funny. Also, it won't keep the momentum going."

Mamrie is trying to explain to me how to build a comedy show. It's early 2013, and we are sitting in Grace's place in LA brainstorming ideas for a live show we're doing together. Grace was my friend from New York who'd just moved to LA and we'd filmed a handful of videos together, and then one year during a convention she introduced me to her friend Mamrie. Mamrie was the daughter of an actor, but she had carved out her own career by using wit that was as sharp as her cheekbones. She'd spent eight years as a bartender before creating her show *You Deserve a Drink*, in which she pairs puns with pop culture references. Mamrie had also studied theater in college, had experience acting and performing, and had survived the rough and ragged New York comedy scene.

I was secretly afraid of her.

Mamrie Hart (and yes, we share a last name, what the fuck) was everything the world thought I was. Funny and clever and talented and confident. I was just waiting for everyone to realize that she was the real deal and that I had no idea what I was doing.

I was an Internet kid, but Mamrie was a theater kid, so all of the things I was confused about in terms of performance, she was an expert in. And since the concepts behind our shows were so similar, I would have expected Mamrie to absolutely hate me.

But she didn't.

In fact, she was a considerate person, an excellent cook, and a funny, caring friend. Slowly and casually a friendship between us formed. Everything seemed as though it was going to be just fine until Grace and Mamrie suggested that the three of us put a live comedy show together (AKA my nightmare).

Grace and Mamrie had been performing together for years at the Peoples Improv Theatre in New York. From there they had gone on to do other projects together (Bloody Marathon, the launch of *You Deserve a Drink*, and so on), so creating a live comedy show was a formula they knew well. But my entertainment experience was making videos for my channel, and I had absolutely no idea how to take an idea and make it into something fit for the stage.

In that brainstorming session, my suggestions all seemed to be falling flat. For people who work in and write comedy, brainstorming ideas with other comedians is par for the course. But as a newcomer to the craft, I took every critique and bit of negative feedback like a direct attack on my fragile sense of self. I already felt as though I was in over my head in Los Angeles, and now I was working with my friends, whom I so desperately wanted to like me, and I was so clearly letting them down.

The whole situation made me feel frustrated. Which made me

feel emotional. Which made me feel angry. Which caused me to just shut down.

So our early brainstorm sessions were short and uncomfortable.[3] But I pushed through and tried to take the criticism and instruction as best I could without feeling so embarrassed that I wanted to abandon the project.

Weeks later we had our very first #NoFilterShow at the Nerd-Melt Showroom, a comic book and comedy venue in Los Angeles. I haven't watched any videos from that first show. I actually don't watch any of our shows. I've noticed that Grace and Mamrie always do, and that's part of their method. Reviewing their performance and looking for improvement. But that's not the way I work, and it only leads to self-derision.

The show came and went with little emotional devastation, and thus it was a total victory! Mamrie and I had compromised on my advice-giving idea by coming up with an act called "Carrot Therapist" in which I would go onstage in my carrot onesie, take questions from the audience, and answer with puns while tossing a handful of baby carrots into the crowd. I think it helped a lot of people get to the root of their problems.

With the first show under our belts, we had a second show coming up in the same venue. Our friend Tyler Oakley (now also a prolific online personality) was going to do a guest spot, and we knew he'd be adorable. After one successful performance, I was actually starting to get excited.

But then I committed a comedy club faux pas. A beginner's mistake.

We were discussing the show in Grace's living room, and Mam-

---

3   Just like me!

rie was talking about her bit the night before, something that involved an old woman yelling (I could look up what the bit was *exactly*, but that would involve watching the show online, and again, I just can't bring myself to look back yet). Mamrie and Grace were talking about the dynamics of the show, and I had something I wanted to contribute.

"For Mamrie's bit, maybe they should turn the mic down because it was really hard to hear. Or maybe you should yell less, Mamrie? That way it's not so screechy."

Mamrie looked at me as though I had just insulted her family's honor. She burst out laughing and said, "Grace, *Hannah* is giving me a *note* on my bit." Her reaction left me feeling as confused as I was embarrassed. I wanted to leave, I wanted to cry, but since I was trying to be professional and productive, neither of those was an option, so I just kept my mouth shut.

Grace immediately stood up and started humming to move away from the topic as quickly as possible. Which is Grace Helbig for "Let's not talk about this." We kept our meeting going, but I felt as though whatever step I had taken forward the night before, I had just taken twenty steps backward in one breath.

Later I asked Grace what I'd done wrong, and she explained that it's better not to give anyone notes on their performance unless asked for them. I'd had no idea because I had received so many notes from the two of them—but then I realized it was because I had been asking for them. Duh.

The second show came and went and was even more of a success than the first. It felt better and smoother, and I started to think that maybe live performance was something I could learn, just like you can learn a language. At the end of the second show we all went out for flaming margaritas and celebrated having two shows under our belts and talked about the possibility of more.

At some point I made a joke at the table and Mamrie laughed so hard she cried. I felt as lit up as the inside of the flaming tequila-filled lime in front of me. I took a snapshot in my mind of that moment and vowed to remember it anytime I was letting my shortcomings keep me from moving forward.

Mamrie and Grace were teaching me a new form of social etiquette, the social etiquette of working with other creative people and performers. And I still had a lot to learn. There were many embarrassing moments to come, from choking onstage when we were in Boston to forgetting lines and forgetting props. Getting better took *time* and *patience* and above all *practice*. As someone who had always been too afraid to try, practicing ahead of time was the last thing I wanted to do. But I had to. Because I knew my friends were being honest with me when they told me I could. It's about progress, not perfection.

(UN)PACKING A PUNCH

There is something important that I want to write about, and I am not sure how it will be received. But I'm trying to write from the heart, and sometimes that means breaking through the surface of what's comfortable.

Hrm. Maybe that's a bad analogy for starting off a chapter about self-harm.

Let's try again. In this chapter, I'm trying to write the truth, and the truth isn't always a lovely and beautiful thing. But I believe it's important to reveal.

That's better.

Okay, so here it goes:

I want to be a role model. I want to be a good role model. I like to hold myself accountable to the community around me, and I strive to be the best version of me that I can be.

I meet a lot of teenagers and young adults at my events. Hundreds, even. Over the course of the *Hello, Harto!* Tour, I would say I met close to a thousand people. Not all at once mind you, but if there were roughly one to two hundred people at an event; with twenty-two events, that makes—woah. Actually, that's way more than a thousand. Math!

Anyway, when someone arrives at the front of the line, we have these thirty-second encounters that can get emotional. For both parties! I like to hug and thank people for sharing their stories and their journey with me. It's lovely. Truly.

And sometimes, though not too often, people come up to me and tell me about their experiences with self-harm, and then they ask me if I can sign their scars or if they can just show them to me because they feel my videos are helping them to stop hurting themselves. Then, with my consent, they politely show me their scars/scabs and we do the hug and the photo and everything is fine and dandy like sour candy. I say, "Good luck, you're doing great!" and they are on their merry way.

But other times, people are more passive about showing me their scars. And I'm not a fan of that.

For example, let's say someone is wearing long sleeves, and then, while handing me something to sign, they pull up their sleeve to show me their fresh, glistening cuts, staring me directly in the eyes waiting for my reaction. Obviously I see them, but if they don't say anything about it, I don't say anything about it and I just sign whatever it is and tell them to have a nice day.

But the truth is that this is a real trigger for me, and honestly, I don't know what I'm supposed to do or how I'm supposed to respond. I feel trapped and helpless.

Look, if you're stuck in a cycle of self-harm, please ask for help, from a loved one or professional. But ultimately you have to help yourself. Because really, the only person who can save you is you.

NOVEMBER 2007

Naomi asked me if I'd been punching things lately. I told her no. She said she was glad to hear it.

I had started putting cigarettes out on my arms though. But I didn't tell her that.

By the time I was a freshman in high school, things at home had gotten bad. Mom's psychotic episodes were growing more frequent, and since we moved into a better neighborhood the cops had started to come more often when called. Maggie was growing faster and faster, and in many ways a toddler is harder to manage than an infant. Especially one as smart and vibrant as Maggie. She was getting hard to keep track of, and she was starting to have thoughts and opinions and to vocalize them. Once, when my mother pulled her pants down in the kitchen to laugh/scream about something while looking at her crotch, Maggie ran into the room in her pull-ups and said, "You're crazy! Hey! Listen! Stop it!" in a voice that was as loud and authoritative as a three-year-old could muster. She was already a force to be reckoned with.

Then I'd walk Maggie back into the living room and restart whatever VHS she had been watching. We'd sit together for a little bit before I'd go back into the kitchen and see if there was any chaos that I could control.

I have a thousand memories like those, but only once, when I was a senior in high school, did everything change.

That morning I woke and walked to the kitchen to discover that there was broken glass on the floor. Orange juice was everywhere. What a waste of good concentrate.

David came in and told me to get dressed quickly because the cops were coming. I asked where Maggie was, and he said she was fine, but that I needed to hurry up and get dressed because my mom was really pushing it this time. The neighbors had called the cops again; they had already come by the night before, and now they were on their way back. David looked desperate and tired.

I walked back toward my room, which had been Naomi's room. Technically the room was part of the garage, and a drywall divider had been erected to make it into something resembling a bedroom. Naomi was home from college because it was winter break. It was separated from the main house by three small steps that led to a concrete floor. The wall that we built was thin and white and hollow on the inside. One of the original walls had a hole in the bottom, possibly from some incomplete construction. I liked it, though, because there were holes in the wall where ivy crawled through from outside. It was always cold, but I liked the cold. It was the best room in the house during the summer. The door to the room was made of hollow plywood, and there was a hole through it. The hole was in the shape of a fist, my fist. I can vaguely remember punching it because I was frustrated with Naomi for locking the door. I couldn't understand why I didn't get to share the new room with her and I actually scared myself a bit when my hand broke through. Naomi opened the door, and then both of us were laughing. Mom came down, and at first she was mad but her anger quickly dissolved into her telling me that it was actually quite impressive, that I had such incredible strength and we should really find a way to enroll me in martial arts![1]

I've still got a scar on my knuckle from where the plywood splintered into my fist. I told my friends it was from opening a tuna can, though I don't think anyone had actually asked about it. I probably pointed it out because I wanted someone to notice that something was wrong, but I didn't have the words to talk about it.

Most times when I punched walls, there was nothing to see except for the skid marks on my hands. Sometimes I wouldn't punch at all, I would just press my fist against a surface and lean forward with my full body weight and as slowly as I could drag my knuckles down or across. Any marks that I left could be wiped away. I did that a lot.

My other favorite release was to look in the mirror and hit myself. That started in elementary school. First thing in the morning when I was alone and already late or I knew I hadn't done my homework the night before, or I knew there was a quiz and I was having trouble understanding the material that would be on it, I would look in the mirror and hit myself. I wanted discipline. I wanted punishment. I wanted rules and attention. I'd look myself in the eyes or down at the sink and rap the base of my hand against my face until

---

1 We barely had our act together enough to get to school with a decent attendance rate. Anything extracurricular was a daydream. It was a nice thought, though.

instinct told me to stop. I was fair skinned and bruised easily, and once a teacher asked if there was anything going wrong at home. Before I could reply she told me that if she ever felt I was in danger she'd have to notify Child Protective Services. I told her of course I understood that, but that everything was fine. After that I avoided that teacher, whom I'd previously hung out with after school. I felt as though she had betrayed me somehow by threatening to call the police on my family.

On the day that everything changed I stood in front of the hole in the door for a long time, wondering if Maggie would one day end up punching things, too. The thought made me incredibly sad. Things had gotten worse since Naomi left for college. I couldn't handle this on my own and one day what would happen? Would I leave Maggie behind and go to school somewhere, too? What was my plan?

I realized I didn't have a plan for the future. But I could have a plan for the present.

I decided to go back to the kitchen without changing. Technically, I was already dressed because Naomi and I had always slept in our clothes. David telling me to go get dressed meant "Go put on your cleanest things and find a toothbrush and smile." It meant "Go put on your mask and get ready for the show."

As I approached the three steps back to the house, I stopped to pray. I prayed that today would be different. That somehow today, when the cops came, they would stay. That Maggie's future would be different from mine. That she wouldn't live in a house with holes in the walls. That I wouldn't have to keep living with holes in the truth. When I finished my prayer, I saw a police car pull up and a young officer get out. By that point we recognized most of the officers who came to the house, but this guy looked new. There was a sliding glass door between the house and the driveway, and I saw

him in the moment I passed it. I didn't tell anyone what I was doing. I just opened it and walked outside and asked him to stop for a
second and told him the truth.

He listened and then called into his radio for social services and
more officers. He then moved past me and kept walking toward the
front of the house. I felt sad and sick. I had broken the only rule we
had. I had betrayed my family.

From there the betrayals got worse. After more cops arrived
and my mother was taken to the hospital for a seventy-two-hour
hold (obviously not her first), the social workers and police officers
spent a long time talking to David in front of the house. His expression was empty. He seemed as though he was giving up. I kept
waiting for everyone to leave. I didn't know what was happening
or what was going to happen. Then David turned and went inside
and left me and Maggie standing there on the lawn. Someone told
Maggie to come with them and I went to follow, but a social worker
stopped me. Maggie asked if I was coming with her. The social
worker stepped between us blocking her from my line of sight. I
remember that she was wearing a gray suit. She seemed in control.
She turned to me and told me to tell Maggie that we would see each
other again in a few days. On Wednesday. I asked her if it was true.
She said nothing. But her expression showed I had no choice.

I bent down and hugged Maggie and lied.

I didn't see Maggie again for three weeks. In the foster system, they
can't determine who from the biological family is "good" or "bad,"
so the blanket rule is that there is to be no contact between the removed child and relatives. Maggie and I broke the rule by meeting
at a Starbucks with the help of her new foster mom. She had radiator

burns on her arm. She told me that one of the other kids had pushed her and she had fallen into the radiator. I comforted her as best I could trying not to let my own grief show. We called them tiger marks, and I said she was like a fairy that lived in the jungle.

I can't describe what it was like to see my baby sister that day, knowing that she was injured and there was nothing I could do about it, that I would have to send her away again. In many ways, I felt as if Maggie were my child, because I had raised her up until that point. I can't think about those days without crying. It's a loss that still feels present even though now I can call Maggie or see her anytime I want. The guilt I feel over that moment—though I know it's unfounded and there was nothing I could do—still feels like a wound that hasn't fully healed.

The nights following that visit, my already restless sleep became impossible. I couldn't stop thinking about Maggie in an environment totally unknown to me. My heart was breaking at the thought of what I'd done. I'd torn our family apart. My memory was already changing. Had it really been that bad? Had I made the right call? What if I was imagining things? Reality wasn't always what it seemed.

During that time, punching walls wasn't an option. We had a court date that we were working toward, and I had to testify. I needed to be the best I'd ever been. A shining pillar of wellness so that I would be allowed to have unmonitored visitation with Maggie. I couldn't sit in front of the courtroom with bruised or bleeding hands or cuts on my arms. So leading up to the court date, I had to find more subtle ways to hurt myself. And I did. But I don't want to share them here. I don't want to give anyone who's struggling any ideas.

The court date came and went. I wore a gray button-down and a black pencil skirt I'd borrowed from Rachel. The shirt was too tight

across the chest, and the buttons pulled as I sat in the courtroom trying to look as grown-up and put together as possible. All the while the
woman who was the subject of the hearing, my mother, stared at me
with a smile on her face and a look of total disconnection behind her
eyes. I was grateful for her inability to comprehend reality in that moment. I don't even remember if David was there that day. Ultimately,
it didn't matter. The trial went as well as it could have gone.

Maggie was placed into the home of a family of a close friend
and former boyfriend of mine. The family was kind and open-
hearted and doing their best. Eventually, they adopted her and she
had her own family and her own journey to begin.

It was also decided that I would live with Rachel's family for the
rest of high school and I started my application for emancipation.
The requirements to declare emancipation are:

1. You must be at least fourteen years old.

2. You do not want to live with your parents. Your parents
   do not mind if you move out.

3. You can handle your own money.

4. You have a legal way to make money.

5. Emancipation would be good for you.

Literally. That's it.

My application was accepted, and I went to live with Rachel's
family. I was going to finish high school and graduate with my
friends and even be able to have visits with Maggie. Everything was
hunky-dory.

Except for all the unresolved pain on the inside. Whoops. Forgot about all that.

As time went on, it became clear that things were not okay. My friendship with Rachel was dissolving because I was self-destructing. We had been like sisters, but now we were less than friends and I wrongly felt like an unwanted roommate and a charity case. I hated who I was.

Senior year of high school, I started smoking. Not only for the chemical effect but because it made me feel even more disgusted with myself. It reminded me of my mother and my stepfather who both smoked and whom people looked down on. Now that I lived in Rachel's house, where someone might notice marks on a wall, I started using cigarettes to burn the hairs off the top of my hands. And then up my wrists. And then, if I was alone and could get far enough, I'd press a lit cigarette into the skin under my bicep. Just enough to turn the skin pink. Only once did I press down far enough to make the skin blister and leave a scar. But it was easy to cover. And this self-conscious teen was not into tank tops. Hiding your wounds is at the core of self-harm. I did it not only to prevent the world from seeing that I had a problem but to prevent myself from seeing it, too.

It wasn't until college that my recovery began. My worldview expanded. I met others who'd been through pain and who had come out the other side, and I didn't feel so alone. I began to care for my well-being in a way I'd never tried to before. Before then, I don't think I'd ever tried to care for myself at all.

But the healing was slow, and there were many times when I relapsed. Scraping my hand or punching the wall or my head when I was in pain was like an instinct. I didn't have any other tools to process my emotions. In order to change, I had to actively unlearn the reflex. It was incredibly tough.

I never spoke to a professional about my problems in college. And it wasn't until I went into therapy as an adult that I was able to make some real progress. But I took baby steps on my own that helped a little. If you're curious, here's what they were:

* **Want to love yourself.** That was step one for me. You have to want to love yourself first, and then you learn the ways to do it.

* **Do something different.** I had a professor who I was very close to in college tell me that when he was young, every time he wanted to cut himself he would drop to the floor and do push-ups. I started doing that, too. Bonus! Now, I've got great arms.

* **Get away from your tools.** For me my tools were walls and mirrors. If push-ups weren't enough, I would go on a walk to get away from my tools. I would also walk where I knew other people were going to be because I certainly wasn't going to punch anything in public. And if I noticed I was starting to scrape my hand along

a fence, I would cross the street to avoid it or walk faster.

* **Reading over bleeding.** There are many great books out there on self-harm. I recommend finding one that speaks to you. *Freedom from Self-harm* is one that really helped me.

* **Above all: talk about it.** Talk with people you love and trust. Talk to a medical professional.[2] The best help I ever got was going to therapy to heal the wounds under the surface. To forgive my family and forgive myself.

So there you have it! I have never discussed my journey with self-harm publicly, and frankly, I'm still on the road to recovery. These days when I start to feel myself floating inside my body,[3] I stand up and start moving around. Or I take a walk. Or I count colors (something my friend Kati Morton recommended). The hardest thing is being in the car when I'm triggered because I don't know how to distract myself. In that case, Kati recommended shouting as loud as I could. I do that sometimes. But it startles me a bit.

In those moments of relapse I know that I need to be patient. So what if I have a triggering experience and I end up slapping the steering wheel? Or if I'm exhausted and angry and can't calm myself down? The worst I might do these days is slap a wall or a counter-

---

2 I know therapy is a privilege that depends on money and time, but if you *can* get yourself to see a professional, you deserve to give your life your best chance.

3 This feeling is called disassociation. I would disassociate from my body during times of trauma, and then the only way I could pull myself back would be to injure myself.

top. It stings, but it's better than burning myself with a cigarette or punching walls. I'd say I've come a long way. I always have to try and remember to be kind to myself.

It's a journey of continued effort and occasional failure. And that's okay.

I can't beat myself up for that.

PUN INTENDED.

NEST

In the last chapter we talked about the last day I spent at home with what was once my family. Now I'd like to tell you a bit about the homes I make today.

I've made it pretty clear that Los Angeles isn't my favorite city. If I weren't in entertainment, there is nothing on God's green earth that could keep me here. I much prefer cities that are cloudy and cozy and comfy and cultured. Not that LA doesn't have culture! It does, in its way—I've just had a hard time acclimating to it.

After living in LA my first year, I seriously considered moving back to New York, but my therapist said that if I couldn't be happy in one city, what made me think I would find happiness in another? I told her that I would give LA another shot, but this time on a month-by-month basis. No commitments.

I probably would have left a month after she and I had that conversation—if I hadn't met someone.

In early 2013 I finally gave in to the fact that LA is an industry town. I actually made a New Year's resolution to get out there and meet more people and not be so averse to networking. I suffered through more than a few deadly cocktail functions, and then one day a friend invited me to come along to a birthday party for a fellow industry person whom I'd never met. The function actually sounded pretty cool—a private party at an artisanal cocktail bar I'd been wanting to check out in newly hip downtown LA. I brought my childhood friend Hannibal as my plus one, and as soon as we walked into the party I was introduced to the birthday girl. Francesca was petite, with dark hair and bangs and catlike blue eyes. I was smitten.

We chatted periodically through the night, and at one point I told Hannibal that I had the distinct impression the birthday girl had been hitting on me. He looked over at her, a vision in silk and leather, and then looked back at me: a short, frumpy dump of a homo wearing a flannel shirt and a beanie to cover my hair, which hadn't been washed in a little too long.

"Uh. No. I don't think so, dude."

Midway through the night, we left the party to go get breakfast for dinner at a diner I loved called Fred 62. And though the party was behind us, I couldn't shake the feeling that something was coming up ahead.

A week later, Francesca and I awoke in my bed, partially undressed and mostly confused. We got up and went out for coffee, and we got to know each other a bit. She told me she was straight, and I told her I wasn't interested in dating.

Both of us were lying, but only one of us was lying to themselves.

Francesca worked as a publicist, and a lot of her insights helped me to build my career into what it is today. It's the power of love, you guys. Makes people compromise. I compromised by going along with some of the aspects of Hollywood that I didn't enjoy, and she compromised by encouraging my "crazy" ideas that nobody was interested in. Between the two of us, we found a shaky middle ground and moved forward together. But about a year and a half into the relationship, I told her I couldn't stay in the closet with her any longer. She wasn't ready to come out, and that was her business, but I personally found it to be too painful after so long. So in October 2014, I ended our relationship. Or tried to. Ultimately, I was too codependent and we ended up a couple again before long.

Francesca and I built our careers together, but our relationship wasn't just about nurturing each other professionally. We really loved each other. At the same time, we each had our issues: I was often moody and angry, and she was often unhappy and detached. Spoiler alert: that's not a healthy combination. But Francesca was my first real girlfriend. She knew everything about me, she understood my work, and she even comforted me at night when I had panic attacks in my sleep. That was not an uncommon occurrence. I'd sometimes wake up choking, unable to move. Francesca would hear my panicked breathing, wake me, and gently say, "It's okay, it's okay." I'd apologize and she'd go back to sleep, and I would get up and give up on trying to rest. Clearly I wasn't my best self when we were together, but maybe that was as good as it was going to get for me. Maybe I would never sleep well at night. Maybe I would never feel safe in my own home.

I'm the type of person who moves into a new place but never

unpacks the cardboard boxes. I just pull my belongings out as I need them. I buy books and bookshelves, and armchairs for reading, but that's pretty much it. Pre-Francesca, walking into my apartment you wouldn't have found any art on the walls, but you'd have seen a stack of frames in a corner waiting for "someday" to hang them. You wouldn't have found a TV or any plants, either. The rooms I'd lived in had always been about function over form. A stack of books, a chair, and a mattress on the floor. Oh, and a camera, and a couple kitschy items for the kitchen. I wasn't accustomed to material things, and frankly, they intimidated me.

So when Francesca suggested that she move into my place, I readily agreed. Francesca was so sophisticated, and I knew she would make our home beautiful. Once she moved in, there were never any dirty dishes in the sink and the house was always clean. Incredibly clean—Francesca's cleaning patterns were very similar to my stepmom Jenny's, an observation that Naomi made one Christmas. And clean meant healthy, in my mind.

Not only was Francesca very clean, but her family had always been very big on tradition, and so was she. Another foreign concept for me. Francesca and I shared two wonderful Christmases together. On the second one we were unboxing her family ornaments, the same ones we'd pulled out the year before, when I looked over at her and asked, "So we celebrate Christmas the same way—*every* year?" She looked back at me, equally shocked but smiling and shaking her head because she was getting used to statements like that from me. That comment, and many others I made over the course of our relationship, showed her how far I was from understanding "home" and "family" the way she knew them.

Material things were second nature to Francesca. I don't mean that in a bad way! The woman had great taste. Her parents were wealthy and exotic and European. Decorating the house, buying furniture, going grocery shopping, those were the tasks that she could perform effortlessly and that daunted me completely. With no frame of reference for making those kinds of decisions, walking into a department store and thinking "What do we want for the house?" rendered me silent and panicked. I'd look at Francesca wide-eyed and say, "You pick. I have no idea."

So Francesca would pick, and we made a home together. Or rather, two homes. The first place we lived in together was cozy and humble, but ironically, as we encountered more problems in our relationship, the urge to move into something more opulent grew. We both ran our businesses from home, and we were constantly stepping on each other's toes. Maybe it wasn't emotional space we needed. Maybe we just needed more physical space! Yeah. That was the ticket!

In November 2014, we moved into a house that I can only describe as a little absurd.

It had two floors, vaulted ceilings like a fancy log cabin, and a deck that wrapped all the way around with a view of Los Angeles that you see only in movies. Not to mention the pool out back and a detached studio for me to work out of. It was perfect for two people who liked to play just as hard as they worked. In that house we threw parties a couple weekends a month, parties that usually ended with Francesca in bed with a migraine and me trying to convince people to jump into the pool with me at 4 a.m.[1]

---

1 I usually managed to get people into the hot tub, but only a brave few wanted to jump back and forth with me between the two.

The house was massive, and it took us a while to furnish it. Francesca would mark off weekends on the calendar labeled with areas of the house that she wanted to finish: "FLEA MARKET—rugs, couch for downstairs, something for Hannah." It was sweet, and she was trying, but I wasn't, and every weekend I would find an excuse to bow out of these field trips and spend the day getting high and feeling detached.

The truth was, I had my own tastes and opinions on what I wanted in our home, but I didn't know how to voice them. Not to mention that spending money like Francesca did made me feel self-indulgent—and guilty. My mother was living somewhere in squalor and possibly in danger, and there I was looking at a couch with a four-figure price tag that Francesca declared "reasonable for the quality." I felt as though she were speaking another language and that I wasn't speaking at all. I felt dumb and insecure. It was a feeling that reminded me of many humiliating memories growing up, and so to avoid it I would drink and detach.

Which is how I found myself most weekends in our gigantic house with a pool and a white dog and my own separate studio, standing in the kitchen in the afternoon and drinking straight from the bottle. This didn't feel like happiness, but I figured my idea of happiness was distorted to begin with.

Francesca encouraged me to do things "for me" and to get things "that I wanted," but it felt impossible. I bought myself a Wii, and in the middle of setting it up I started to cry, walked over to where she stood in the kitchen, and told her I felt so guilty for all that I had. I was so worried about my mom. Francesca didn't know what to do. I was a wreck. Francesca and I were entangled and enmeshed and had no sense of self outside each other. We were caught in a web of our own design, neither of us strong enough to break free.

We stayed that way for two and a half years before I finally got up the courage to clear it all away.

In December 2015, almost a year after ending things with Francesca, I called Naomi and told her that this was the year I was going to risk it and try to save Mom. She'd been living in the small apartment we'd found for her in 2008 in a low-income area of East Palo Alto, but we knew she needed to be hospitalized. The trouble was, forcing a move like that on an unstable person is very risky. On the advice of our father, we hadn't pushed for hospitalizing Mom in the past. In his opinion, trying to get her some help could lead to her running away from us—that had been his experience in the past—and from there she would be homeless again. Or we could give her a key to an apartment and let her spin inside until everything in her stopped spinning entirely. His stance was that there were only two options:

* She dies in the apartment.

* She dies on the street.

It was a no-win scenario. The best we could do was to make our peace with that.

But I don't have a lot of peace in me. I have a lot of unrest. So when I called Naomi and said, "I'm doing this no matter what," she understood and agreed to help. I saw a tarot card reader (no joke) to help me pick a date when the stars would be aligned and we could forcibly hospitalize Annette. The woman drew the cards from her deck and immediately told me, "This card stands for the beginning of Taurus. End of April, early May."

Now, believe what you will about astrology, but having a deadline in mind helped me organize myself into action. I chose to focus on preparing myself for April 26. That was the day we picked.

I got myself back into therapy (I had stopped going for a couple of years), but this time, instead of "talk" therapy, I tried cognitive behavioral therapy to help me break free of my harmful patterns. It was supereffective for me. I strongly recommend it for those who may be interested.

I also started going to the gym, maintaining healthy friendships, and setting boundaries between my personal life and my professional life. Then I got to work building a case with the help of my friend and fellow YouTuber Kati Morton.

Kati is a good soul. She's a licensed marriage and family therapist and has worked in psych wards in the past. Her role was to help me gather and document the evidence we would need to prove our case "against" my mom. I know this sounds strange, but it was our only option. The mental health care system in this country is so broken that the only way to get someone help in the form of hospitalization is to build a detailed case proving him or her to be mentally unstable, even if that is already abundantly clear.

I was applying for what is called LPS conservatorship[2] of my mother, which is basically impossible to gain unless the mentally ill person has physically attacked someone (within recent history) or

2 LPS conservatorship is a process in which the court appoints a person to make certain legal decisions for another person. Or, as my mom likes to call it, "adult adoption." The difference between LPS and probate conservatorship is that you can hospitalize someone for mental illness against his or her will.

has attempted to take his or her own life (again, within recent history). There is no way to be proactive and save a life. The laws are designed to function retroactively after a violent incident.

And frankly, I didn't want my mom involved in a violent incident.

But Kati and I discovered that there was another way: if we could get a hospital to declare her *gravely disabled*, it could give us a referral letter from the attending psychiatrist to begin our petition for the LPS. However, step one of this process would still be getting Mom arrested and forcibly admitted to a hospital. How would we do that?

Her delusions had gotten worse, and her ability to act on them was increasing. She was banging on neighbors' doors, screaming at them to release her family members (she was convinced that her dead father was being held hostage by one of them). She also regularly called apartment security to have them come and protect her from the convicts waiting outside her door. For the first few years she was in the building, security humored her, but ultimately they stopped taking her calls. The management office we rented from often asked me to remove her, but when I explained that I couldn't and begged them to let her stay, they backed down. To remove her they would have had to call the police, and we'd deliberately found her an apartment in a low-income immigrant area, knowing that the neighbors and managers there would be unlikely to call the cops. And no one ever did. But now the only way to get her into that hospital was to have her arrested. So we'd basically wedged ourselves into a corner.

One night in March, my mom called me twelve times in rapid succession around 3 a.m., saying that her friend was planning to shoot me with a gun. I needed to know so that I could protect myself, but she said that maybe she should get a gun first.

Bingo.

When Naomi and I drove up to visit her in April, we called the police and reported the incident.

The police went to her apartment and asked her if she planned on shooting anyone.

"No," she replied.

The officers called us back and said, "That's good enough for us!"

Naomi took the phone from me and told them that she was terrified our mother was going to hurt someone. That they must take action now. Because they had the power to save lives, and not all dangers are ones that you can see right away.

"Have you ever been afraid of someone you love?" she asked.

Whatever magic Naomi possesses worked. The officers took Annette in and we gained a three-day hold, which meant that I could get into her apartment and take pictures for evidence. Sure, we had incident reports, court cases, voice mails, and e-mails and statements from family members, and many, many documents in our arsenal, but as someone who works in a visual industry, I knew that photographic evidence would be crucial.

"I hope it's dirty enough," I said to Kati as we drove over to Mom's. Naomi wouldn't be joining us because she had meditated on it and had a sense that she really needed to stay away. We follow instinct in our family, so although I questioned her decision, I didn't argue with her about it.

"Even if it's not, maybe we can find something that will be useful in building the case. Has your mother ever been a tidy person?"

I thought only a moment before replying "We should probably go by the hardware store first."

"For what?"

"Face masks."

Standing outside the apartment door, I thought about the last time I'd been there, almost two years earlier. Francesca and I had flown up one summer day to visit Maggie and her family. We were blissful and still in the fairy-tale phase of our love. Francesca was the only girl I'd ever introduced to my mom. Naomi and I weren't speaking at the time (she was going through a divorce and had "run off to a mountain"[3]), but when Francesca met Maggie they instantly adored each other. I was feeling pretty good and decided that since we were up there she might as well meet my mom, too.

All things considered, from my perspective, the visit went really well. Sure, Mom was ranting, and sure, her tiny studio apartment was a sty, but hey, it wasn't the worst. From my perspective.

During the visit, I sat on a bench my mother had salvaged while Francesca sat perched on the edge of the couch (another dumpster find), barely moving. She had her hands folded in her lap, and she

---

3   Naomi had been trying to heal from her PTSD and as part of that process felt she needed a dramatic amount of space from the Hart family and Mom. She wrote a letter to one of my aunts outlining the reason for needing to cut off all contact with them in order to heal. At the time, she thought that would be a lifetime. She didn't give me a heads up about this, which stuck me in the middle of a family debate that I wanted no part of. For a time, it was even difficult for the two of us to talk, and we became distant. After she had taken time to heal, she came back into my life and we reconciled. More on that in the next chapter.

was staring at my mother so intently that I assumed she was simply trying to follow along with her tirade. Sitting on the bench, I faced my mom while she stood and spoke, gently pacing back and forth, her eyes glassy and her face red, but with no objects in her hands and no urgency behind her words.

After we left I got into the car and smiled. "That was the best it could have gone! She was having a good day."

I looked over at Francesca, and her face was stark white. "Let's go," she said.

I started to drive, and Francesca was silent. I let her stay quiet for a bit, but after a mile or so I pulled over and asked her what was wrong. She started to cry and reached out for me. Through her tears she told me that she'd been so scared that *"that woman"* was going to hurt me. She loved me, and she'd been sitting right by the lamp because if *"that woman"* was going to attack me, she knew she could fling it at her and we'd be able to get safely out the door.

I was shocked. "Really? You were that scared?"

Now it was her turn to look baffled. "Hannah." She held my face and stared hard into my eyes. "You *cannot* go back there. Please promise me you'll never go back there alone."

"I can't promise that. I mean, what if I need to see her?"

"Then see her in public." Francesca was emotional and adamant; it was an unusual tone for her. She wasn't one to let her feelings show when she spoke. She wasn't one to let her feelings show, period. In that moment I never felt so loved but also so scared. Francesca's desire to protect me was so sincere that it shook me to realize how blind I was to how ill my mother had become.

"Promise me."

"Okay."

"Say it."

"I promise."

I'd kept my promise. Now, almost two years after that conversation, I was about to step into that apartment again. I had actually forgotten all about that conversation with Francesca. But as we approached the door, Kati asked, "When was the last time you were here?" and I remembered.

"You ready?" I looked at Kati, and she gave me a latex-covered thumbs-up. We both had gloves and face masks on. I was grateful we'd opted for the extra protection, because as we approached I noticed some bugs crawling along the windowsill. The blinds were broken in places, but it was pitch black inside except for the light of a small screen that was playing *Parks and Recreation.*

"Cool. Okay! Here goes." I turned the doorknob and entered.

The first thing I noticed was that the air was warm and humid. Familiar.

"Oh, my god."

I heard Kati whisper behind me, but there was nothing more to be said. The place was rotting from the inside. We were there with a job to do. I needed to take those pictures and go. There was no time to stand outside and take it all in.

As we entered, the cockroaches on the floor scattered toward piles of garbage, where they could stay shrouded in darkness. I took a wide shot with my camera. Click. Dust and insect shells covered every surface. Click. Her hoarding had continued in the time since I'd been there, and there were piles of books and miscellaneous objects ("treasure") everywhere. Click. There were also jars filled with dark brown liquid, overflowing with cigarette butts. Click.

"Coffee."

"What?" Kati asked. I didn't realize I had spoken out loud.

"Sometimes she puts cigarettes out into her coffee. She doesn't drink the coffee once it's cold."

"Oh—okay."

I turned to look at Kati. She hadn't made it past the threshold. I had somehow made it into the center of the room, having followed a path through the filth that was wide enough for the single air mattress that was slowly deflating in the corner. I felt as though I was missing frames in my mind. When had I walked into the room? I thought I had just opened the door.

I felt really hot. I was sweating, but didn't know why. In one of the missing frames I must have entered the room and was now covered in sweat. Memory is weird. Good thing we had pictures. Click.

I started using the flash to reveal the yellow stains that had formed on the walls. Click. Probably from cigarette smoke.

"Do you want to turn that off?"

Parks and Recreation was still playing on the screen. I forgot, and looked around for a remote to turn it off. I pulled open a drawer, and dead cockroaches rolled around like marbles. I took a picture and shut it, surprised to see that the roaches were dead. Maybe she'd bug bombed the place once. Good for her. Maybe she wasn't as sick as I'd thought. Click.

Everything was covered in dust and cockroach excrement, so instead of continuing to look for a way to shut off the TV I just unplugged it. There were boxes and boxes of old newspapers and empty beer bottles. Click. I didn't remember my mom ever drinking beer, to be honest. Click. Then I noticed a pamphlet from the Asian Art Museum. I had gotten her a yearlong membership for her birthday, and maybe that meant that she'd gone. I almost smiled. I'd smile about that later. I felt oddly robotic. As though my hands weren't attached to my body but I still controlled them. They weren't responding as quickly as they normally did. I felt as though I was floating. Everything else was slowing down.

Kati was still in the doorway, "I think you should just take a couple more—maybe just of the kitchen, okay? Then I think that you have enough."

"Okay."

"I'm really surprised that there aren't more flies in here," Kati said, covering her face-masked mouth with her sleeve, "considering the amount of rotting food."

"That's what the spiders are for," I said automatically, moving toward the kitchen to take the pictures we'd need.

Kati looked confused. I pointed up.

Katie gasped. The ceiling was covered in cobwebs, speckled with black dots of spiders and their prey. A ceiling fan turned slowly, its movement having carved out a track in the webs that surrounded it. That would be a good photo. Click.

"Oh, my god. Oh, my god."

I almost laughed. "What, you're afraid of spiders?" I asked, feeling casual. I tried to walk into the kitchen, but my feet had stopped working. Odd. I snapped a picture from where I was. Click. What's floating in that bowl? Who cares? Click. "It's not that hard for me to be in here. Honestly, this is just like the house I grew up in."

Kati's face fell slightly, but she regained herself. "Make sure you get a picture of the floor."

"Good call." I crouched and took a picture of the floor. You could see a path about ten inches wide where Mom paced. Click.

I noticed an electrical plug on the floor and realized the fridge was unplugged. She did that sometimes. Something about the "frequency of the transmissions" coming from the fridge. Sometimes she would actually unplug the fridge in the middle of conversations so she could pay more attention. That had led to many expired surprises when I was a child. I remember being little and trying to drink milk as soon as it was bought, while it was still cold and sweet, before it got chewy.

"Hannah, I think you've got enough."

I looked up. "The fridge is unplugged. I'm sure everything in there is moldy. Lemme get a shot of it, and then we'll go."

There was just one problem: I couldn't really move my arms. I was confused. And frustrated with myself. I stood there and stared at the handle of the fridge. Arm, go. Hand, go. Just lift and open. Open the fucking door and take a picture.

But my hands stayed at my sides. I was on pause. I kept staring at the handle of the fridge, begging myself to just open it. I could smell it. I knew that if I opened the door, I would get a picture that would seal the deal. Just fucking do it.

But my body was betraying me. It refused to obey. I was stuck.

"Hannah?"

I looked toward Kati. My eyes were unfocused, but I could see her figure in the light pouring in through the door. The light that scattered the cockroaches. She held her hands up in front of her as she stepped into the apartment itself. "Are you okay?"

"I'm fine."

"Okay are you going to take a picture?"

"I kind of can't."

"What do you mean?"

I felt blank. I didn't know how to explain. "I . . . can't. I'm trying, but . . . I can't."

Kati, a trained mental health professional, probably understood far better than I did how deeply I'd been triggered.

"I can feel the skin on my face," I said, "but I can't move my arms."

It was true. I suddenly had a very odd sense of awareness of the skin covering my entire body. But I couldn't move.

Kati marched forward and touched my arm. It felt so foreign. "I think we're done, okay. Do you want to go?"

I didn't want to go. I didn't want anything. I was silent.

"Hannah, I think it's time to go. Are you ready?"

I couldn't answer. I didn't know what to do. Should I try to open the door? I wished Naomi were there. She was always so good at making decisions.

"I don't know." I knew my face was blank. I felt blank.

My phone pinged. It shocked me a little, and I lifted it out of my pocket, thankful to see that my hands still worked. I pulled off my glove and swiped. There was a text from Naomi:

Text me as soon as you're finished. Just get what you need. Don't linger. Don't stay.

Naomi and I joke about how there's a psychic link between us. That we feel moments when we need to reach out to each other. This was one of those moments.

"Yeah, let's go." Kati was out the door in about three footsteps. I turned for one last look and thought about taking the art off the walls. Mom's sketches and drawings were yellowed and cracked, cobwebs gently dangling across them. There was even a painting Maggie did in kindergarten. They hadn't seen each other in twelve years, but somehow she had kept it. I moved to touch it, and a cockroach scuttled out from behind and grazed my hand. I felt that.

I started to feel everything.

I pulled my hand back, and my stomach wrenched. My face was itchy. My neck was itchy. I'm allergic to cockroaches. Why could she never remember that? I'm allergic to cockroaches, and they give me rashes. Why didn't she care? Why didn't she notice? Their dust makes it hard for me to breathe. I choke sometimes when I try to sleep.

I was filled with grief and rage. The place was disgusting. I wanted to burn it down.

I left the apartment and slammed the door shut behind me, my knees weak as I walked down the stairs and toward the car. If I stopped moving, I thought I might collapse.

I drove us back to Naomi's in silence. When Naomi asked, "How was it?" I replied, "I think we got enough." Kati told her about the spiders, and Naomi closed her eyes and told her she used to kill the ones near our mattress on the floor. I said I never remembered seeing that many spiders. Her eyes welled up, and she hugged me. "I know you don't remember spiders, honey, but do you remember spider bites? We were covered in them."

"Oh." I remembered. Naomi had a system with a needle she'd use to get the venom out. I had little green scabs on top of the swollen mounds. "Spiders are what make spider bites," I said flatly, as if the two facts had just clicked together.

She nodded, wiping a tear. Patient but sad. "That's right. That's why we kill spiders or put them outside."

"But what about the flies?"

"We don't have any flies, Hannah. We have clean houses now. With no spiders or flies."

"Oh."

Sometimes it's hard for me to remember that, too.

The photos I'd taken proved to be the most compelling evidence we had in our case against Mom. It was worth the trip for that reason alone.

But more than that, the trip had changed my perspective on my own habitat. It had made me realize that certain habits I had weren't about nature at all. They were the result of nurture. Or neglect.

The court case would take about a month. Weeks later, I had to drive back down to LA for a press day I couldn't miss. I was reluctant to go, even though there were chunks of time that passed when there was no work to be done on the case. I called Francesca from the road. She'd left me a message earlier that week from the Creator Summit, a yearly event for the YouTube elite that I had to miss. What had made it even harder was not being able to explain why. Everyone just assumed I hadn't been invited. I was no longer elite.

But what can ya do?

We talked for forty-five minutes, and I told her all about the apartment and the spiders, and she was sympathetic and a good listener and also proud of me. It felt really good. I told her I was excited to get back to my own apartment and hang some pictures. She laughed. We didn't speak often, our breakup policy having been to give each other as much space as we needed for as long as was needed. Sometimes it's just not that healthy to talk to an ex.

I thanked her for all the patience she had shown me, and she thanked me for all the love I'd shown her. I asked her if she was working on her personal stuff, and she said it was none of my business, and then I started to ask her about self-care and she told me to stop. I apologized. She sighed and said she knew she needed to but didn't want me to nag her. I told her I wasn't nagging, just expressing my opinion. It was tense but then we both paused and laughed.

"Gah. We really haven't changed, huh?"

She sighed. "Yeah . . . you know, I think that was really the problem with our relationship. There was always a lot of love but not a lot of respect."

I agreed. "I'm working on that. Trying to treat myself with respect."

"That's good."

We got off the phone, and I finished my drive. After three weeks in the Bay Area, I never thought I'd be so happy to come home. I surprised myself as I opened the door to my house in LA, a door that led to clean hardwood floors, a record player, and boxes of board games and art above the fireplace. I loved the place. It was clean, and it smelled like cedar candles. This was my home. And my home was not a reflection of madness, but of myself.

FABLES

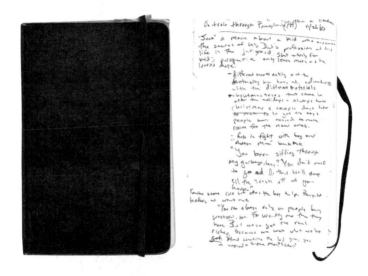

ON TRAIN THROUGH PENNSYLVANIA (PA) 11/26/10

"Junk" a movie aboul a kid who uncovers the secret of his Dad's profession and his life in the junkyard. Shot entirely from the kid's perspective, [audience] only learns more as he learns more:

* *different scenes acting out the fantasies he has, and adventures with different materials [from the junkyard]*

* *Christmas trees that come in after the holidays—always have*
  Christmas a couple days later to get the toys people have tossed
  away to make room for the new ones

* *Gets in fight with boy at school over "Action Man" backpack/*
  "you been sifting through my garbage, hey? You don't need
  to go and do that we can drop all our trash off at your house
  instead."

Teacher seems cold but offers the boy help. Recycled binders and
what not.

[Dad speaking]
"You can always rely on people being wasteful, son. For wanting
more than they have. But we've got the real riches here, because we
want what we've got."

My earliest memories are all of Naomi. In those memories, she
is telling me stories.

My very first memory is of lying on a blue carpet, and as I lift my
head I see a line of My Little Ponies all in a row. Naomi is pointing at
each of them, I don't understand what she's saying, but I know that
she is describing each of them and they are having a parade. Naomi
must be about four years old in this memory and I must be approach-
ing one, because the only house we ever had with a blue carpet was
the one my parents shared when they were together. The memory
ends with Naomi looking up behind me as I am being lifted. I'm being taken somewhere and leaving the ponies behind.

When Naomi and I would lie in bed at night on our shared mattress, I'd ask her to tell me stories to fall asleep. I'd interrupt with jokes or my own ideas, and we'd laugh and would soon be telling the story together, but when it came to a happy ending, Naomi always told it best.

Our childhood revolved around making up stories and games. Once, for Christmas, our Grandpa Joe (our mom's dad) gave us *Star Trek* action figures. They were the coolest of cool. We would take them on "away missions" and make up stories about the alien planets we visited. We'd pile them in the center of the room and divvy them up, each of us choosing one character at a time. The only rule was that you had to play each character in your pile at least once. I never got tired of those games.

Another memory: Naomi and I were looking for something to eat, and we checked the freezer. Sometimes there would be an old bag of bread in there covered with ice crystals that could be fixed in the microwave. We found a bread bag in the freezer, but inside there were dead kittens. The family cat (a wild thing that strayed into and out of the house) had given birth to a litter, but some had died. When I asked Naomi why there were kittens in the freezer, she told me a story about how Mom was saving them for all of us to bury in the backyard.

When we got older, Naomi started writing her stories down. Everyone said she was a beautiful writer. She also wrote poetry and won an award for her writing at school. I was jealous.

One year Naomi saved up from her part-time job at a place called ChickN-ChickN and bought herself a guitar. She started playing music and writing songs. She listened to lots of Pink Floyd and Led Zeppelin and wrote a song she performed at our school talent show. She was so good, it got written up in the local paper. But I didn't celebrate with her. I was angry and resentful because she always seemed to be out living her exciting life and I was focused on our baby sister, Maggie. I thought she should have spent that money on the family. That's what I would have done. Naomi told me that we all make choices. But I didn't feel as though I had any choices left in the wake of hers.

As we entered young adulthood, the bitterness I felt toward Naomi grew. She left for college and left me behind. Going away to college was the right decision for her, but again I resented her for it. Naomi and I have always been opposites, we're like fire and water, but I wanted us to be on the same page. What I didn't realize back then was that we need our differences for balance. If we were the same, we'd never be able to confront the challenges that faced our family.

So when I set out to tell you guys about the relationship between myself and my sister, I couldn't think of a moment that could be emblematic. There were too many moments. It was in all moments. I was formed in response to her, as she was formed in response to me. We were each other's parent and each other's child.

I thought about the incident with the kittens, I thought about the incidents in the summertime, I thought about how once our mother broke a wooden paddle hairbrush by repeatedly beating it against her own head and screaming "This is how much pain I'm in." And how Naomi and I looked at each other and laughed because we'd had the same thought and could see it in each other's eyes: "That was our only hairbrush."

So as you can see, all the stories I tell and have told include Naomi in some way on the other side.

So instead of telling you guys about the ways Naomi and I had to learn to work together to try and save our mother . . . I'd like to tell you a story about a general and a monk.

THE GENERAL AND THE MONK

Once, long ago, there were two children born to a woman in a cave. The Woman loved them, and cared for the children as best she could, but the Woman had magic in her, not good magic, not bad magic. Just strong magic.

Before the Woman could learn to control the magic, it overtook her and turned her into a Witch. She tried to hide the magic from the children, but they could see it for themselves. The Townsfolk in the Village below began to gossip about the Woman because her magic was strong, but you never knew which way it would turn. Sometimes she would bring chaos and burn the fields of others, but sometimes she would bring laughter and light and paint pictures of the village for the children. They began to call her the Good-Bad Witch.

The Townsfolk had names for the children too: the Crying Child and the Quiet Child.

The Crying Child would ask the Townsfolk for help when the bad winds would turn. But they could not help. They would not help. The Quiet Child was quiet but listened.

The Crying Child would plead with the Townsfolk for bread, and they offered whatever they could. The Quiet Child was quiet but grateful.

The Crying Child would fight the Witch, crying out against her magic, demanding that the winds cease as they stormed, but it would only add strength to the spells. The Crying Child was helpless. The Quiet Child was quiet but helpless, too.

Years passed, and the Good-Bad Witch grew wretched with madness. The Townsfolk wouldn't speak to her; they were afraid of her and unable to understand her ways. Eventually, even on days when the good winds would blow, the Good-Bad Witch was avoided. Treated like a monster by all except her children.

But the children grew, and it soon came time for them to leave the cave. The Quiet Child was reluctant to go. Who would travel to the Village to get supplies for their mother? The Crying Child told the Quiet Child that there was nothing to be done about it. And the Quiet Child grew loud and angry. "Go, then! We will be better off without you! You want to leave because you are weak. I am strong enough to stay, but you should go. You only make things worse."

Wounded by the madness of the Witch and the anger of the Quiet Child, the Crying Child left the cave and wandered into the world alone, their heart broken in many places. *Perhaps I am weak, they thought. Perhaps I have made things worse. Perhaps I have abandoned the Quiet one. Perhaps I have failed them both.*

The Crying Child wandered through many different Kingdoms, far from the cave of their birth. They learned of many people and many ways. They learned that there was much pain in the world, not just their own. And they learned that there was also much Joy. It wasn't that Life had selected their family to suffer, but rather that in Life there is both Suffering and Joy.

The Crying Child found a Mountain where others who had suffered had gone to learn to live through letting go. They learned that one must not struggle to change the unchangeable. That the only peace to be found is the peace of acceptance. Away from the chaos of the Cave, they were able to quiet the passions of their heart. On the Mountain, in constant meditation, the Crying Child found peace and became a Monk, devoting their life to teaching others about life after pain and suffering.

Years passed, and the Monk would sometimes hear news of the

Quiet Child. "Is that so?" the Monk would say, smiling peacefully before moving along. Sometimes the Monk would think of the Good-Bad Witch and would feel the pull of family deep in their chest. But the Monk would not allow themselves to be pulled apart by this feeling and would instead sink deeper into meditation.

One day, the Monk was sitting in meditation when there was a knock at the door of their hut. They rose slowly, leaning on their staff to stay grounded as they opened it.

The Monk blinked in the sunlight and saw a General dressed in brightly polished armor, with arms folded across a shimmering chest plate. The General also wore a helmet, and the Monk instantly recognized the voice that rose from beneath it:

"The Good-Bad Witch is dying. Her magic has consumed her."

"Is that so?"

"Yes. She is dying, and I cannot let her die like this."

"We must all die one day."

The General's fists clenched beneath the metal mesh gloves. "While you are correct, dear Monk, we can all make choices while we live. I choose to try to save her, so that I can live knowing that I have done all that I can."

The Monk sighed and closed their eyes. The General spoke again, firmly: "I don't expect you to understand, here in this hut hidden away from the world. But I must tell you that I have traveled far and wide and I have gathered the resources of many Kingdoms. I have grown great in wealth and knowledge. I have led and I have commanded. I stand here before you, informing you of my quest and offering you a place by my side."

The Monk could suddenly picture the well-worn cord that joined their hearts. Damaged but unbroken. They could sense hope and fear in the General's words. There was much passion behind them, but that passion was fueled by the fires of pain. The Monk knew that the General could not win this battle without help, without seeking balance. Perhaps this journey could show them the way together.

The Monk stepped outside and shut the door, turning to the General to say, "You're not so quiet anymore."

As they traveled together down the Mountain, the General informed the Monk of their quest. The first phase was to hire Mercenaries from the Village to take the Good-Bad Witch to a Healer in a Far-off Kingdom where the General had Allies waiting. As the magic of the Good-Bad Witch had grown stronger and more violent, they had been seen by many local Healers, but those in the Village could hold her powers for only three days. It was believed that the Healer in the Far-off Kingdom was very powerful and would be able to hold the Witch's power for longer.

The Monk listened to each phase of the plan, replying gently, "Is that so?" and nothing more. The General grew impatient and demanded an explanation for the Monk's lack of urgency. In response, the Monk shared many lessons of patience and peace with the General as they journeyed homeward. The General didn't understand them but found them interesting nonetheless. As they approached the Village, the General put their helmet back on, explaining "No one knows that the General is the child of the Good-Bad Witch. I'd like to keep it that way."

"Is that so?" the Monk replied coolly.

They enlisted a Sherpa whom the General trusted who would accompany them on the quest and who could cool the General's temper whenever they grew angry with the Monk's apparent apathy.

The General understood that the Monk was peaceful, but did they have to be so smug about it?

The group prepared for departure. The Mercenaries gathered, and the General gave the Good-Bad Witch an elixir that would cause them to sleep through the length of the journey. But early on, the plan began to fall apart. Sometimes Mercenaries like to exercise their power in strange ways, and instead of leading the group to the Far-off Kingdom, they suggested a shortcut, leading to a Kingdom Across the Water. They had no Allies in that Kingdom, and there wasn't much time before the elixir would wear off and the Good-Bad Witch would awake.

The fear in the General's heart turned to anger and the anger to hopelessness, triggering a spell that the Witch had placed on the General long ago, to keep them close, reducing the General to the Quiet Child they had once been.

The Monk and the Sherpa peered under the General's shining helmet, but their armor looked empty. Then, suddenly, the Monk could see a small child nestled behind the chest plate, hoping to remain unseen. The Monk moved to face the Quiet Child hidden inside the armor. The Monk gently knocked against its front, asking if they could speak.

The Quiet Child made no reply. The Monk spoke.

"Hello, little one."

"I want to be left alone," the Quiet Child said with bitterness.

"Is that so?" the Monk asked. "Have you spent much time alone?"

"I've been alone for years. Alone because of you." Hate dripped from the child's words.

"Is that so?" the Monk asked again.

"You left me because you were too weak to stay in the cave. You were too weak to stay, and you didn't try to take me with you."

"Did you want to leave the cave?"

"No! Of course not. But you shouldn't have left, either."

"I see. Are we the same, you and I?"

"Not at all." The child stood suddenly, pointing a finger in the face of the Monk. "You are weak. And I am strong. We are not the same at all."

"You are right. We are not the same. I couldn't stay in the cave with you because I was not as strong."

The child was confused but didn't want to show it. "You should have stayed, because out there everything hurts!" They began to weep. "I know, because I did it, too. I left, and now that I'm back, I'm in even more pain."

The child fell into a crouch, banging their head against the armor for being so foolish and hopeful.

The Monk spoke in a soothing tone, unmoved by the child's tantrum. "You are right. This world does hurt—"

"See! So—"

"You have turned your pain into passion and drive, yes. But it is still pain."

"So don't tell me to go back out there! It will only cause more pain. If I hide in here for long enough, eventually I will sleep and the pain will stop."

"The pain will not stop. It will resume upon your waking. The answer is to learn to confront the pain and embrace it."

"What good will that do me?"

"There is much in this world that hurts us, but if we let pain become our master, we live our lives as slaves. Do you want to be a slave?"

Tears ran down the Quiet Child's face. "No, but nor am I a master."

"You are right. You are not a master. You cannot lead because you are still a child." The Monk smiled at the Quiet Child, removing the helmet to wipe the tears from their face and moving to embrace them. "Thank you for trusting me and for showing me your grief. There will be pain to come, but you are not alone and you never have been alone. I am here with you."

The Quiet Child let themselves be held, pressing their face against the worn fabric of the Monk's robe. And suddenly the spell was broken.

The General stood, lifting their shield as they spoke. "There is still hope. We must still try. I'll find a ship to carry us across the water."

The Monk stood and said, "I am ready."

I believe that each of us has the power to change the world in a thousand small ways, without even knowing it. The person who changed our world was a receptionist at Fremont Hospital who recognized me in the waiting room.

When the police arrested Annette in April 2016, they took her to the San Mateo County General Hospital for a three-day hold. Naomi, Kati, and I spent the day sitting outside the locked doors to the psych ward ER, waiting to speak with the doctor on call. He was finally able to see us at the end of the day, and we told him about our mission to get the LPS referral letter. We pleaded our case, showing him our documentation and telling the story of thirty years of suffering, Naomi and I each taking turns when the other couldn't speak. Eventually, our passion and our perseverance won out, and he said that he understood and would admit her.

But then they transferred her to a different hospital, Fremont General, without even telling us. It was a fluke that we found out. We jumped into the car and raced to Fremont, where the new attending psychiatrist would not see us. We were told we could leave a message. Naomi and I refused to leave and were preparing for an all-night vigil when a nurse on staff told us there was no use waiting. The doctor had actually left for the day hours earlier. As we stood in the lobby, quietly debating our options, the receptionist recognized me and asked if there was something she could do to help.

That woman saved our mother's life . . .

I explained what was happening—that our mother had been brought in on a 5150 (when the police arrest someone and admit them to the psych ward at a county hospital for an involuntary seventy-two-hour hold) and that she had been transferred from San Mateo County General Hospital to Fremont without our knowledge. Apparently, the rules for communicating with families for psych emergencies are different from those for medical emergencies. In a psych emergency, the hospital is allowed to contact next of kin only at the request of the patient. But what if that patient (my mother, for example) is babbling nonsense? Good luck getting a phone number out of that situation. Not to mention the sad fact that many facilities don't even try to contact family because there is none. Many people suffering from psychosis have been abandoned by their loved ones because of the difficulties of dealing with the illness. (I'm not judging the families in these situations. I'll admit that I've considered abandoning my mother many times; it's very difficult to try to help someone who can't be grateful and who doesn't believe that they are sick.)

She could see how much we had been through, and the gift she gave us was to go behind closed doors and find the social worker who had been assigned Mom's case. She came back out and said "You have ten minutes."

We spoke to Dennise, the social worker, and presented the case we had gathered. We told her about our goal of conserving our mother, which she discouraged us from pursuing because it was such an unlikely outcome. I then asked her to take a look at our catalogue of evidence and at the very least recommend the psychiatrist get a 5250, a fourteen-day hold, which would give us the time we needed to gain the referral for the next step.

Dennise hesitated and asked if our mom had any insurance.

I was confused by this question and said, "No, of course not. She's terrified of paperwork."

Dennise then began to explain why gaining approval for the 5250 was unlikely and recommended we take our mother to a shelter. I had flashbacks to trying to take her to shelters back when I was in college, only to have her grab the steering wheel of my car to try and crash it.

At the mention of a shelter, my systems shut down. Blessedly, Naomi's didn't.

"We can pay the fees if you keep her. The county will not be responsible. I will sign her up for Medi-Cal today, but you *must* keep her here. We have money. We have lots of money."

I was embarrassed and moved to silence Naomi, who had literally shaken her purse to emphasize her point. But then I looked at Dennise and realized that in fact it was about money. Money was the issue.

"Is this really about the cost?" I asked with blunt naiveté.

Dennise's response was simply "The county is paying for your mother to be here. There is a lot of scrutiny, but I think with insurance and with this case history you've brought, we may have a better chance at a 5250."

Translation: *Yes, it's about the money. Thank you for shaking your purse.*

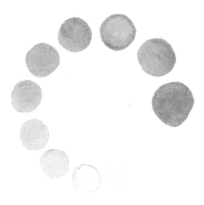

I remember walking out of our meeting with the social worker, having won the battle for the fourteen-day hold and reaching out for Naomi's hand, a childish instinct but my instinct nonetheless. I would not have been able to move forward without her. My passion keeps me going, but sometimes it also grips me too deeply and I shut down. My pain and my passion are intertwined. But in Naomi's pain she has sown the seeds of patience. And so we are able to pinch hit for each other.

When Naomi cut ties with the family to heal herself, I was so angry with her for leaving me. But the truth is, she was there all along. Our parents hadn't been there for us (one due to illness, the other due to ignorance), and we'd been left to fight for our survival. Naomi had needed to leave because she knew she could not survive if we were chained to each other. We had to free ourselves from those ties to keep from sinking.

During the period of time we spent in the Bay Area, fighting our mother's case, we started calling each other the General and the

Monk. It was our way of forgiving each other and understanding the adults we had become: a General powered by passion, a Monk cultivating patience in the face of pain.

This was our way of leaving our child selves behind, and buffering into adulthood. Choosing between the pixels we'd like to fully load, and which broken images are better left behind.

EPILOGUE

I spoke to my mother today. I won my case as conservator[1] and was able to relocate her to a facility that is helping to rehabilitate the mind she has left. They say she's incredibly high functioning and that while it's too soon to know what shape recovery will take, it still might be possible. She's also been on medication for the longest she's ever been on meds. She's speaking to a therapist and psychiatrist on a weekly basis. Her paranoia is contained, but her delusions are as strong as ever. Still, with the medication, she feels less urgency to act on them. When I talked to her, she sounded like a different person. She asked me questions like "How are you?" and remembered the things I'd mentioned to her in a previous conversation. She asked me how this book was coming along. She told me she loved me. That she was proud of me. She thanked me for saving her from being a bag lady.

After we hung up, I sat on the floor of my kitchen staring into my hands. I couldn't tell what I was feeling? It felt like shock, but I didn't feel empty—I felt full.

I was full of joy.

I know that these may seem like tiny, insignificant things, but

---

1   The county official who filed for me stopped me outside and said "This never happens."
    I replied "This needs to happen more."

to me they mean the world. Having a mother with even the vaguest sense of a shared reality is a gift I never thought would be returned. Living my life without wondering if she's covered in cockroaches or threatening the safety of another human is a relief that I cannot express in words. The conservatorship will only last a year, but a year is a long time compared to all the days we've lost.

It does make my heart feel heavy though, to think of the woman she might have been, had she gotten the proper treatment for her illness early on. I want to show you a drawing she once did—she'd call it a freehand pencil "doodle"—that reminds me of that lost potential.

Over the past ten years, I've processed a lot. I'm still processing. And there is more to be done. But I'm very proud of the person I am today. I'm proud to be gay. I'm proud to be a reckless optimist. I'm proud to keep learning and sharing what I've learned. I'm proud to be a work in process.

As we end this time together, I'd like to show you the reason for my decision in December 2015. What gave me a final nudge in the direction of the impossible hope. What made me call my sister and tell her that I was determined to fight the odds and accept that I might fail but at the very least try to beat the system to help our mother. To be fair, there were many reasons: the love and support of my online community, the love and support of my friends and found family, the love and support I had learned to show myself. But this discovery tipped the scales from daydreams and hope into planning and action.

It was something I never saw coming: a small package that arrived at my house on Christmas Day, nearly thirty years after the Christmas of 1987, when my mother was first taken away.

CHRISTMAS 2015—A GIFT AND CARD FROM NAOMI:

To Our Dear Annette,
For her birthday, June 19, 1981
Love, Grandma and Grandpa Hart

This is a book that my great-grandfather Hart gave to my mother. It was written in 1936 by his brother, my granduncle Henry Hart, who was one of the first scholars to translate ancient Chinese poetry into English.

And here is the Christmas card that accompanied it in the mail, from my sister:

Dearest Hannah,

In addition to very many warm things, I've included a package sent to you through time and space: a birthday gift to our mother when she was 22, before having children, before the Witnesses, from our Great-Grandparents. I'm sure they'd want you to have it: a treasured keepsake from our collective past. An Heirloom.

Wishing you a warm and joyful year,

Naomi 12/21/15

And now let us welcome the new year,
full of things that have never been.

Rainer Maria Rilke

Dearest Hannah,

May you find Happiness
Throughout the Coming year.

In addition to very many warm things, I've included a package sent to you through time and space. A birthday gift to our Mother when she was 22, before having children, before the Witness, from our Great-Grandparents. I'm sure they'd want you to have it. A treasured keepsake from our collective past. An Heirloom.

Wishing you a warm + joyful year,
Naomi 12/21/15

READ THIS TOO

(Please read this! Please please please!)

I want you to know that I didn't win LPS conservatorship because winning is common or possible and all you have to do is try. I won because of the following advantages:

1. **I'm white.** This is an advantage. We can't deny it.

2. **I'm educated.** Both Naomi and I have high-level degrees, which means that the intensive research it takes to understand a complicated legal and medical system is more accessible to us than it is to many people.

3. **I'm healing.** I've gone to years of therapy, and I take medication. Both Naomi and I have PTSD from a childhood of trauma. It's hard and triggering to even talk to our mom, let alone display our trauma in front of impassive third parties who have the authority to simply say "No. Your pain isn't good enough. Let her shoot someone first."

4. **I'm wealthy.** What paid for my years of therapy and medications to help me excel? Money, dudes. Fucking money. I have it. I've saved it. I'm using it to fight this case. And you know what else money buys you? *Money buys you time.* I spent three weeks in the Bay Area fighting the system. Naomi's schedule isn't as flexible as mine—she was able to take only a week off from work— but otherwise she telecommuted.

And the icing on the cake:

5. **I'm famous.** People are endeared to me, as I am to them. I have a community that is rooting for me to win.

Still, with all of these resources, I almost lost my mother and could still potentially lose her. So let me ask you this question:

If a white, wealthy, educated, famous person can't save her parent from the streets—who can? Who does this system work for?

The system works for itself.

So there you have it. The system is broken. It's been broken since the LPS Act of 1969,[1] which basically outlines the protection of "patients' rights" but leaves no room for people to help those who suffer from debilitating paranoia and delusions that prevent them from acknowledging their own illness. The act is out of date and based on nonscientific ideas and assumptions. It needs to be updated to reflect our current understanding of debilitating mental illnesses. It doesn't

---

1 For more information on the LPS Act of 1969 and all of the problems it has caused for the mental health care system, check out the Treatment Advocacy Center's website: http://www.treatmentadvocacycenter.org/ component/content/article/194.

take into consideration that many people with severe mental illness can be treated and achieve some sense of normalcy for their lives. Though diseases like schizophrenia are not curable, they are treatable. And that's a huge difference.

So the system is broken. And broken systems create broken families and broken lives.

There is also a deep stigma surrounding mental health that is directly responsible for many of the violent crimes and senseless deaths that we hear about in the news. Every time there is a shooting and we blame the person for his mental illness or his family for not "doing something about it," I'd like you to remember the stories I have just told you and the facts I've presented to you.

We do not have to have the number of homeless people on the street that we have. We should not teach our children that so many people are homeless because they have failed in society.

The truth is that society has failed them.

Our society is stuck between problem and solution when it comes to treating mental illness. We cannot find a solution until we agree on the problem. And it is my humble opinion that the problem is fear. Fear of the unknown, fear of the misunderstood. Instead, let us seek to pursue knowledge over fear. Let's find a way to save lives that can be saved.

A wise woman once told me, "Another word for fear is intelligence."

So let's get brave, and let's get smart.

Thank you for listening, and if you'd like to know more, here is my personal list of readings and references that may be helpful if your family or someone you love is encountering struggles similar to mine:

HANNAH'S LIST OF READINGS AND REFERENCES

I'm Not Sick I Don't Need Help: How to Help Someone with Mental Illness Accept Treatment by Xavier Amador, PhD.

Driven to Distraction: Recognizing and Coping with Attention Deficit Disorder by Edward M. Hallowell, MD, and John J. Ratey, MD.

Anger: Wisdom for Cooling the Flames by Thich Nhat Hanh.

No Death, No Fear: Comforting Wisdom for Life by Thich Nhat Hanh.

The poetry of Rumi.

The poetry of Mary Oliver.

Good Poems for Hard Times, selected and introduced by Garrison Keillor.

Letters to a Young Poet by Rainer Maria Rilke.

Art and Fear: Observations on the Perils (and Rewards) of Artmaking by David Bayles and Ted Orland.

—Hannah Hart, October 2016

AFTERWORD

Writing a memoir and putting your story out into the world is a nerve-wracking act. It's basically like handing a total stranger your diary to read. So I was more than a little shocked by the positive response I got—the number of people who read my book, related to it, and who gained some measure of wisdom or wellness from it. People praised me for writing it—for being a survivor, and for being brave enough to share my story so that others might benefit from it.

But the thing is, I didn't feel brave as I was writing this book. I felt terrified.

I've never been more nervous about anything in my life. I was scared that I had done a disservice to my family and to myself by opening up these chapters of our lives and retelling them the best way I could. What if my memory was too biased to be true? What if I had just made everything up? What if I am a butterfly that's just dreaming it's a human!?

Blessedly, none of that was true. (Except for the butterfly bit. TBD.)

When my sister Naomi called me after reading this book and said, "Good job, boo. Really really good job," I felt relief. And then more vulnerability. Now, it really was *all out there*. What if no one ever looked at me the same way? What if I never looked at myself the same way? I also wondered, now that the deep, formative events of my life had been put to paper, did that mean that the process of processing was over? Was there nothing more to be learned? Nothing left to say?

I went on book tour and each day was a cycle of validation and depletion. It was incredible to meet people who shared similar backgrounds, who had struggled with similar things, or who had even just been touched by a simple sentence or two. Writing has always felt like an incredibly important resource for me—a way of grappling with and understanding my emotions. And I'll admit, it's disorienting to think that I've become that kind of resource to others. Especially when I know that I don't have it all figured out—not even close. I'm still waiting for my own internal resources to build, for my self-compassion to fully form, for comfort to become a reflex.

There were also moments when I was on tour that were heartbreaking. I met people who were dealing with some really difficult sh*t. It made me think about how there is so much suffering in the world. Hugging people and sharing your story feels like something, but it's not enough. Nothing feels like enough. At night after my events I'd lie in bed and I'd cry thinking about how there is so much distance between us. We are all strangers on this planet. I knew that people left my events feeling inspired by my words (which is an incredible honor to be sure). But I wanted their advice as well. I wish I could have read their books, too.

It's difficult to accept that people read this book for comfort and advice, because I'm still struggling. I still wake up every day with all the same flaws as I had the day before. If I'm growing, I can't see it. This is why I write. It helps me track whatever progress I'm making.

But I haven't been writing much lately. Or even making videos as consistently. Creatively, I feel like I'm stuttering. Internally, it feels a bit like vertigo. As if the giant cog or gear of my life is shifting, and

I'm running on top of it in the opposite direction, constantly afraid that I'm going to fall off. When I look back on the events of my story I think, "My life has changed for the better." It feels dangerous to even write that sentence. Why can't I just appreciate the feeling? Why can't I let my guard down? I keep waiting for life's sucker punch. I've been talking to my therapist about this, and she says this feeling of emotional vertigo is common in people like me with PTSD. At first she suggested a new kind of therapy called EMDR (eye movement desensitization), which is supposed to be effective for treating trauma. We actually tried it once, but it left me feeling very . . . raw? Angry? Exposed? Tender? All of the above?

I wasn't quite ready for the intensity of EMDR. Instead we're starting with a "mood tracker," a detailed daily log that I keep of my emotions to help me better understand myself, and thus to better understand and communicate my needs. Everything is so jumbled inside of me emotionally that I actually need my therapist to help me figure out which word connects with each emotion I'm feeling. Like I was embarrassed to ask, "What's the difference between 'sad' and 'lonely'?"

I still feel like I'm not speaking the same language as people around me, but I'm working on it. This feels like a journey of discovery, and I wanted to share what I have so far with you:

1. **SADNESS**—For me this means "disappointment." Someone behaves or something occurs in a way that you'd hoped would be different. For example, I felt sad when you were late to dinner. Which sometimes transitions into . . .

2. **SHOCK**—For me this is "numb." When something

unexpected happens, good, bad, or otherwise, I just throw a wall up. It's a disoriented and distant feeling. Makes it hard for me to reconnect. I get distant from myself and thus from the people around me.

3. **LONELINESS**—This one is . . . still a work in progress. And I think a lot of us would agree that this is a tough one. Being bored and lonely are kind of the same feeling for me, which left unattended can trigger my default state . . .

4. **DEPRESSION**—Hey, buddy.

5. **ANXIETY**—This one for me is about anticipation and judgement. Self-judgement. I don't think I'm an anxious person, but I do spend a lot of my time reflecting and trying to assess whether I'm behaving in the right way. I get nervous before parties because I don't think people like me. I still don't think my friends like me. I'm gonna say this might be because I am still working on how much *I like me*. It's a journey. Oy.

6. **ANGER**—For me this comes from being misunderstood. I feel like the way I speak is too complicated. Not in a "high and mighty" way. But just in an unnecessarily complicated way. I feel like I do my best when I can draw pictures or write things down. People look at me like I don't make sense a lot. And when I don't understand them or they don't understand me I get frustrated, which makes me angry.

So what do I do with my emotional log? Am I supposed to turn it into self-knowledge? Do I start setting goals? I want to reset my emotional defaults . . . is that a goal? Oh, and I'd like to be able to feel happy without feeling dread. When I feel safe or content, I tend to get a deep sense of doom at my core. Oblivion is guaranteed. I'd really like to undo that reflex, if that's possible.

I'm writing this while having breakfast in Iceland. I was at a conference in Amsterdam, and a couple of friends suggested that we take a vacation "just for fun." I can't believe that I'm so lucky. It's hard not to feel guilty and undeserving. But I don't want to waste the opportunities life affords me on guilt. I have to push myself into even the most positive goals.

The inn where we're staying (which slightly resembles a La Quinta) is isolated, designed for the best possible viewing of the northern lights, though actually seeing them is contingent on more factors than just the viewer's location (weather conditions, cloud cover, and so on). We didn't get a chance to see them. But for me the best part about staying in a place built with this intention is that there are windows everywhere, stretching from floor to ceiling. And through these windows I can see the ancient landscape: an expanse of black lava rock, some of it covered in moss or frost, dark onyx to ashy. Wisps of sulfuric steam roll in the distance. The cloud cover is ever present and only occasionally ominous. Most of the landscape is bare, but none of it seems barren.

And in my mug of water beside me floats a slice of lemon: a contrast of color floating on a sea of black rock. Bright. Yellow. Joyous.

It makes me think that anything is possible. That maybe there is more to come. That the unexpected isn't always a bad thing.

XOXO,

Hannah Hart

July 2017

ACKNOWLEDGMENTS

The Uses of Sorrow
(In my sleep I dreamed this poem)

Someone I loved once gave me
a box full of darkness.

It took me years to understand
that this, too, was a gift.
—Mary Oliver

First I'd like to thank everyone for putting up with my pretentious ass inserting a poem at the top of my acknowledgments.

Next I would like to thank my publisher, HarperCollins, and the two editors who worked with me to make this book possible. You showed me a great deal of patience and understanding during the creation of this book. Thank you for letting me miss so many deadlines and helping craft this book into the creation it is today. I am very proud of it, and very proud of us.

Thank you to my manager, partner, and friend, Linnea Toney, for taking on bearing of the brunt of my anxieties with such strength and compassion. You made this book possible. Thank you for creating the space I'd need to finish it, and showing such belief in me during my times of exhaustion and doubt.

I'd like to thank my literary agent Jodi Reamer and my team at UTA. Together we do great work. I'm excited for future projects to come. I'd like to thank Helen and all the "Have a Hart Day" City Captains who volunteer each month and bring joy to the lives of those around them. I am honored to be in such good company as yours.

I'd like to thank my friends, family, and lovers who I have had the privilege to walk beside.

Thank you to Naomi, my monk, sister, and friend.

Thank you to Maggie, my sun, sister, and friend.

And lastly, I'd like to thank my mother, Annette, for being the bravest person I know. You inspire me each and every day. You taught me right and wrong and the flexibility in between. You taught me forgiveness and compassion for all God's creatures. And above all, you taught me to never give up. I can't thank you enough for that.